THIS IS THE CITY

Making Model Citizens in
Los Angeles

RONALD J. SCHMIDT JR.

UNIVERSITY OF MINNESOTA PRESS

MINNEAPOLIS • LONDON

Published by the University of Minnesota Press
111 Third Avenue South, Suite 290
Minneapolis, MN 55401-2520
http://www.upress.umn.edu

Library of Congress Cataloging-in-Publication Data

Schmidt, Ronald J.
This is the city : making model citizens in Los Angeles / Ronald J. Schmidt, Jr.
p. cm.
Includes bibliographical references (p.) and index.
ISBN 0-8166-4190-0 (acid-free paper)—ISBN 0-8166-4191-9 (pbk. : acid-free paper)
1. Los Angeles (Calif.)—History. 2. Los Angeles (Calif.)—Social conditions. I. Title.
F869.L857S36 2005
979.4′94—dc22
2004017203

Printed in the United States of America on acid-free paper

The University of Minnesota is an equal-opportunity educator and employer.

12 11 10 09 08 07 06 05   10 9 8 7 6 5 4 3 2 1

THIS IS THE CITY

For Charlie

CONTENTS

Acknowledgments   ix

Introduction: City of Angels   xi

CHAPTER 1   A City of Self-Made Men: Harrison Gray Otis
and Political Imitation in Los Angeles   1

CHAPTER 2   Hollywood in the 1940s: Emulation during
Wartime   29

CHAPTER 3   The Badge: William Parker, Daryl Gates,
and the LAPD   69

CHAPTER 4   More Than Human: *Blade Runner*'s
Model Citizens   101

Notes   115

Bibliography   139

Index   145

ACKNOWLEDGMENTS

In the tradition mapped out by my subjects, I could claim that I developed the initial argument of this work in dialogue with ancient authorities and long-dead Angeleno elites and refined it on my own in locations throughout the city that Otis built—Bunker Hill, along Mulholland Drive, in Hollywood's Musso & Frank Grill, in front of the Los Angeles Police Department's Parker Center. Fortunately for me, however, I never had to be a self-made scholar, and my exemplary models formed a supportive community around this project. I studied with many graduate students at Berkeley who were inventive and dedicated, but two deserve special mention: Jonathan Bernstein and Christine Trost helped me in a thousand ways, from listening to the same anecdotes and arguments many times over to running crucial bureaucratic missions as I tried to file a University of California dissertation from the remote New England campus of Dartmouth College. Their contributions and friendship have been invaluable. Torrey Shanks was a guiding influence on this work from its development as an entertaining obsession in the aftermath of qualifying exams to the filing of my dissertation and beyond, and served simultaneously as friend, editor, and academic model. Catherine Smith's knowledge of Los Angeles, love of Hollywood film, and enduring—at times heroic—support have been central to my ability to complete and even to enjoy this project. I also wish to acknowledge the enduring and cheerful editorial and moral support of Sven Pierre Paret, Scott Lucas, and Ron Yungul, who provided consistent advice, fellowship, and good humor;

and Christopher Harris, whose fascination with the Southland exceeds even my own.

My colleagues at the University of Southern Maine have been unfailingly encouraging and provided me with a course release that was essential to the completion of the manuscript. Terry Quinn, our administrative assistant, provided cheerful production assistance. I have also had the good fortune of working with several classes of talented undergraduates who helped shape the direction of this book; I cannot list all of them here, but Matthew Kaply deserves special mention. The advice of my reviewers from the University of Minnesota Press was extremely helpful. I thank my editor at Minnesota, Carrie Mullen, for her skill, support, and commitment. I am also grateful for the editorial assistance of Jason Weidemann, Judy Selhorst, and Laura Westlund.

I am extremely grateful for the support of my parents and for the example they have set. My work could never have been completed without their love and guidance. In addition to serving on my dissertation committee, Michael Rogin, Lawrence Levine, and Hanna Pitkin served as models of thoughtful and rigorous research and critical theoretical innovation. Michael was an insightful and supportive dissertation chair as well as an exemplary figure in the study of American political thought, American film, and collaborative scholarship. It was my extreme good fortune to have had the opportunity to work with him.

CITY OF ANGELS

A name conceals or covers a thing, and thereby fixes it, making it a "something," rather than an "anything" or "nothing" and stabilizing its identity. In contrast to the spontaneity of the first linguistic act, naming is mimetic. Through mimesis and then naming, man conceals and checks the meaninglessness of his (originary) utterance and existence and responds to the abyss of freedom.

—BONNIE HONIG

This is the city. Los Angeles, California.

—JACK WEBB

When Los Angeles was first settled, it was named in honor of the Virgin Mary. The village of Nuestra Señora Reina de los Angeles, Our Lady Queen of the Angels, was a small, poor, ethnically diverse outpost of a far-flung European empire, protected by soldiers and serving primarily as a way station on the route connecting the Catholic missions that dotted the Southern California countryside. As part of its transformation into an American metropolis, the village's name was shortened. Perhaps this attempt to name the city as an abode of angels has driven the desire to create a mythic history for the Southland; Los Angeles is presented and represented in a variety of media as a paradisiacal city with a modern history that begins with its Fall. Los Angeles is the result of confidence games and real estate booms, swindles and deception.

One classic version of the city's fall from grace, the story of how L.A. got its water, has been retold many times, perhaps most popularly by Roman Polanski in his 1974 film *Chinatown*. Wealthy elites of Los Angeles gambled their fortunes on the growth of the village into a great city;

accomplishing this task required national advertising, the sale of land to people all over the United States, and the provision of water for the new communities that seemed to sprout up overnight. To gain the water, these elites tricked their fellow citizens into passing bond issues for water that did not actually belong to them that would be used to cultivate and develop land that was not actually part of their city. In the theft of the water and tax money and land, the wealthy elites grew wealthier and Los Angeles grew bigger. In Polanski's film, the water conspiracy is discovered by a private detective, who also uncovers murder and depravity among the city's small and literally incestuous inner circle. Having survived beatings and threats, the detective takes a shower; but how do you get clean in water, when water is a symbol of the corruption you are attempting to fight?

The stories of the fall of the city of angels suggest a core, an essential identity, in the founding moments of what is now the second largest city in the United States. Such founding myths are relatively common; they reassure citizens that their civic life is part of a unified narrative, with established rules and established courses of virtue. (Even if a fall from grace is central to the story of the city, after all, it does suggest a moment of paradise that defines the rest of the story.) Attempting to fix these myths and rules in place, multiple generations of Angeleno elites have attempted to define the identity of Los Angeles, and the history of the city is littered with assurances of mimetic veracity. To be able, as television producer and actor Jack Webb frequently promised, to say, "*this* is the city," with complete assurance, was to be able to conjure the defining virtues of the

Private detective Jake Gittes (Jack Nicholson) bathes in corruption in Roman Polanski's *Chinatown* (1974).

city; after that, citizens would only need to follow the blueprint. Indeed, throughout the history of Southern California, political and economic leaders have demanded that the virtue—and perhaps the survival—of the city depends on this imitative civic education. My concern in this book is to examine the centrality of this mimetic tradition in the politics of Los Angeles. I will chiefly discuss three moments in the city's history: the 1880s, when *Los Angeles Times* publisher Harrison Gray Otis provided a new founding moment for Southern California; the 1940s, when Hollywood was at the center of national attempts to mobilize and purify the American public; and the moment of William Parker, the chief of the Los Angeles Police Department, whose vision of Angeleno virtue dominated the streets and the airwaves of Southern California from 1950 to 1992. In tracing the attempt to fix a stable vision of civic virtue for Los Angeles, I will not present a comprehensive history of the city; I will, rather, illuminate a narrative of authority that has served consistently, in the course of more than a century, to delegitimate and undermine a substantive and autonomous politics throughout Southern California.

FOUNDINGS

In Hannah Arendt's etymology, the root of the word *authority* is the Latin *augere,* the augmentation of the legitimate actions initiated by the founders of a state.[1] Southern California elites argued that Angelenos (and Americans in general) needed to be reminded of the authority of their politics by copying a perfectly realized picture of authorized virtue. The presentation and imitation of political virtue is thus an attempt to preserve an authoritative public, the space inhabited by those citizens who can pursue models back to the legitimacy of their founding. In a republic, however, the preservation of public life requires an active political culture. Republics depend for their survival on the active participation of citizens, and the strict imitation of authorized models can limit spontaneous political action. Examining the power of mimetic politics in Los Angeles requires, first, a confrontation of this dilemma, the call for an autonomous politics and a scripted imitation of authorized action, within republican theory.

The work of Niccolo Machiavelli enacts these paradoxical demands. Machiavelli writes in the *Discourses* that the example of excellent individuals preserved the Roman Republic as long as citizens were willing to imitate it and was even capable of restoring virtue to a corrupted people:

> The way to renew [republics and religions], as I have said, is to carry them back to their beginnings; because all the beginnings of religions and of republics and of kingdoms must possess some goodness by means of which they gain their first reputation and their first growth. Since in the process of time that goodness is corrupted, if something does not happen that takes it back to the right position, such corruption necessarily kills the body.[2]

Such original goodness, present at the founding moments of a republic, serves to define the nation; it is the model by which corruption can be averted.[3] For a republic like Rome, this original goodness is *virtú,* which Gilbert translates as "strength and wisdom," and which also carries connotations of autonomy, skill, and manliness.[4] A politics that is *virtuoso* is autonomous and wedded to conflict (Machiavelli, for example, argues that the constant battles in Rome between the Senate and the populace maintained and even increased the *virtú* of that city).[5] To escape eventual corruption, however, the citizen must be forced to recall his own defining excellence; he is led back to the example of the founders, often by walking in the footsteps of outstanding models. According to Machiavelli, the path to vital, autonomous republican politics is, in short, an innovative and an imitative path.[6]

Not all calls for a mimetic politics confront this dilemma. The pure imitator is explicitly following the models that came before; his or her civic energies are expended entirely on preserving a preexisting state of affairs. The mimetic citizen thus follows paths of virtue, with its connotations of an apolitical moral piety, rather than those of *virtú.* Marcus Tullius Cicero, for example, who defined the imitation of exempla as a central political virtue, called tirelessly for elite citizens to take up this duty and to follow models of deference to historical, philosophical, and temperamental excellence. In *On the Commonwealth,* Cicero defines the pedagogical responsibilities incumbent on the exemplary "wise man" that can govern his emotions and thus govern his fellow citizens:

> He has in fact scarcely more than this single duty—for it includes nearly everything else—that he should never abandon the study and contemplation

of himself, that he should challenge others to imitate him; and that by the nobility of his mind and conduct he should hold himself up to his fellow citizens as a model.[7]

The wise citizen does not innovate; he preserves.[8] Virtue is thus something that is conserved and maintained, not independently created.

As dissimilar sounds can make up harmony, as a wise man can employ his reason to control his emotions, citizens should aspire to produce concord in their state by following the model set by the wise. The good Roman citizens, Cicero claims, should thus obey their model in order to cultivate inner individual peace and general social virtue.[9] Good Roman citizens would not attempt to imitate the actions of a founder precisely; they would imitate the reverent wise man whose inner peace enables him to show proper deference to the legitimate authority of civic tradition. The good citizen's model would be most independently active in his own mind, in his contemplation of himself; politically he would act only as a good conservator. Following Cicero's vision of mimetic virtue, citizens would not compete with others. Good citizens would act together to achieve harmony and to preserve a polity that their ancestors procured for them.[10] By naming Rome's defining virtues—its citizens' willingness to endure tribulation, their reverence for tradition, their apolitical harmony among citizens living and dead—Cicero points the way to maintaining the republic's public world.

But why then does Cicero not call on other Romans to imitate the actions of founders rather than to act merely as conservators? If the authority of the founding is to be maintained, as Arendt claims, through the *augmentation* of the actions of exemplary Roman forefathers, then should not the virtuous citizen strive to compete with models of greatness? Some Roman historians of the early empire argued so; they turned from mimesis per se to the concept of *emulation*. Emulation is imitation with a competitive purpose: "striving to copy or imitate with the object of equaling or excelling." The English word is derived from the Latin *æmulatio;* it shares with its root an implication of "lauding" or respecting models while "striving after or up to them" as well as negative connotations of "jealousy, envy, and ill-natured rivalry."[11] Indeed, this is part of the problem of emulation for a thinker like Cicero; competition threatens change, a transformation of social order and hierarchy, and thus the threat of corruption.

The emulator, after all, follows in another's footsteps, but not piously or reverently; one *may* emulate for the purpose of maintaining one's authority, but without question one emulates in order to increase one's share of glory.[12]

Despite its potential for subversive transformation, emulation, too, carries civic responsibilities. In his account of Lucius Quinctius Cincinnatus's rebuke of the Senate in the *History of Rome from Its Foundation,* Livy draws out the public burdens of emulation, the awareness that as one bases one's actions on the actions of others, one also serves as a model oneself: "You are merely copying the mob—whom no one expects to be politically adult," Cincinnatus accuses. "You are taking your cue in folly from the very people to whom you should be an example of political rectitude."[13] Cincinnatus expresses contempt for the mob here, but assumes that the Senate's imitation of the people demonstrates the corruption of a process that can and should be used for better purposes. The republican emphasis on reverence for the founders, and the difficulties of establishing a virtuous independence from them, found expression in emulation, which promised the possibility of gratified ambition in the framework of filial piety.[14]

Emulation is an inherently unstable mode of political imitation, however. The emulator walks a narrow path to excellence, bounded on one side by the conservative passivity of a Ciceronian antiquarian and on the other by the subversive desire to innovate. Indeed, the tension between innovation and imitation suggests an inherent dilemma in the political nature of mimesis. It is impossible to imitate innovation; to copy is not to initiate. One can imitate passive conservators, surely, but how does one *imitate* the radical excellence of a founding? How does one follow precisely in the footsteps of radical innovation, even if one is competitively imitating that model? When emulation is presented as a central part of political fealty, the problem becomes even greater; the dictate that only people capable of doing the impossible are worthy of being citizens suggests that almost any political action is, by definition, unauthorized and illegitimate. And by laying claim to one specific narrative of civic virtue alone, even emulatory mimesis marginalizes other traditions of participation, often brutally. In Los Angeles, for example, the command to serve the city and augment the nation's virtue has, in fact, served as a rationale for narrowing the scope of political life.

The Angeleno elites were following an American pattern. The paradoxical demand that the good citizen simultaneously innovate and imitate has been a central fixture of the politics of the United States since the eighteenth century. The American Revolution provided the opportunity for both a radical new beginning, the founding of a republic, and the mobilization of the population within the mimetic narratives of antiquity. During the war, Samuel and John Adams, George Washington, and others offered a living civic education by emulating Roman heroes and standing as exempla in their own right.[15] Tom Paine promised in the most influential of the revolutionary pamphlets that the North American British colonials had it in their power "to begin the world over again,"[16] but most of the radical Whigs envisioned instead an emulatory return to the "founding excellence" of ancient states. Samuel Adams promised that the United States could be a "Christian Sparta"; Washington, that monarchical subjects could be transformed to republican citizens through his own exemplary struggle to emulate Cincinnatus.[17] By constructing a new public space through the imitation of the ancients, the revolutionaries sought authorization for their radical undertaking and, in Arendt's words, they were right in thinking that they "had to derive the stability and authority of any given body politic from its beginning." As Arendt also points out, the Americans did this in part to ground their actions in the example of an earlier group of founders, outside of the political multiplicity and risk of revolutionary action. The Whigs "could not conceive of a beginning except as something which must have occurred in a distant past."[18]

As Wood has illustrated, however, the revolutionary repercussions of the war outstripped the intentions of the Whigs themselves; the foundations of colonial political and social hierarchies were undone by events,[19] and although they had been extensive at the republic's founding, calls to the emulation of antiquity quickly fell from popularity. The donning of classical personae was deemed unworthy and unrepublican in the early 1800s; the public figure was supposed to act spontaneously as his own nature dictated.[20] This new ideal reflected a growing disdain for artifice and an increasing anxiety that any imitative behavior was inherently slavish mimicry. The new republic, it was hoped, would create a citizenry that "wore its heart on its sleeve," that was "sincere," and that did not pretend to be like anyone else; in the words of David Ramsaye, "In republics, mankind appear as they really are, without any false colouring."[21] The new ideal was not without models of its own, however. The author "Epamindondas" in Tom Paine's *Pennsylvania Magazine,* for example, provides us with a clear picture of the new model that was being forged after the revolution. The public orator, "Epamindondas" argued, should "seem to be free from any embarrassment, hurry or disorder." He had to appear to possess "composure" and "to appear indifferent [to] what the audience thinks of his performance . . . indifferent as to reputation and constrained by a sense of duty." The political orator, in short, needed to learn to appear completely unstudied, to act as if he were not acting. He should not concern himself with the ideal of pursuing his own glory by following the model of citizens of great reputation, or of providing a model in turn. As for the good orator, so for the good citizen; one should strive to appear original and spontaneous, behaving as if one followed no outside models.[22]

Thus the model for American mimesis was spontaneous and unstudied virtue: the good citizen would imitate a model of natural innovation. But how does one imitate radical innovation? By crafting superior personae; those who are best at pretending to be completely genuine are thus able to maintain political authority by being able to bar others from their legitimate place in the political realm. In short, from Cooper's fictional Natty Bumppo to the film-star cowboy president of the 1980s, the master artificers of innovative spontaneity dominated the authorized public world of the American Republic. In the nineteenth century, this shift was marked by the political success of the "self-made man" as a new public model and, paradoxically, by an explicitly unemulatory approach to the American founders themselves. Abraham Lincoln, for example, in his 1838 speech to the Springfield Young Men's Lyceum, argued that the passing of the revolutionary generation required a shift to pious, antiquarian reverence rather than a new generation's attempt to rival the deeds of Washington, Jefferson, and the other founders. "Like everything else," Lincoln noted, the exemplary actors and deeds of the revolutionary era "must fade upon the memory of the world, and grow more dim" and thus "their influence can not be what it heretofore has been."[23] Under the circumstances, a threat to the nation arises from new citizens who might strive to surpass the deeds of the founders, who would insist on treading new ground, for genius "scorns to tread in the footsteps of any predecessor, however illustrious."[24]

This field of glory is harvested, and the crop is already appropriated. But new reapers will arise, and they, too, will seek a field. It is to deny, what the history of the world tells us is true, to suppose that men of ambition and talents will not continue to spring up amongst us. And, when they do, they will as naturally seek the gratification of their ruling passions . . . The question then is, can that gratification be found in supporting and maintaining an edifice that has been erected by others? Most certainly it cannot.[25]

The preservation of the edifice built by the founders has been set and should be preserved, Lincoln argued. One could strive for a seat in Congress or a presidential chair, but one should not compete with the model of the founders; that might endanger the civic edifice. Indeed, Lincoln asserted, the "temple of liberty" must be shored up by "pillars, hewn from the solid quarry of sober reason," as Cicero's wise men attained peace by governing their passions with their reason. And if citizens must imitate members of the founding generation, Lincoln added, they should do it by "pledging their lives, their property, and their sacred honor," in the words of the Declaration, to the legacy handed down from the founders.[26]

Taken at face value, Lincoln's speech seems like a collection of Ciceronian pieties. Nonetheless, Lincoln himself did not eschew the emulatory project. He warned that the ambitious would "burn for distinction; and, if possible . . . will have it, whether at the expense of emancipating slaves, or enslaving freemen."[27] Lincoln, of course, joined the ranks of Washington and the other founders by emancipating slaves, staying within an ideological edifice created by the founders and building onto it. Garry Wills has argued that Lincoln's reading of the Declaration of Independence has shaped the modern reading of that document; grappling with the model of the American founders, the sixteenth president reshaped American political identity.[28] Whereas Cicero urges his contemporaries to show respect for history by merely preserving the work of their ancestors, Lincoln provides a model of active reverence, walking in the footsteps of the founders but redefining their principles of popular self-rule and equality and pushing them further than they had previously extended.

To put it another way: Lincoln altered the course of American political life in a way comparable to that of the revolutionaries, by innovating and yet promising to re-create mimetically what he had found. Within the republican patterns of the United States, successful innovators exist in order to be slavishly imitated, and radical transformation must be defined as a mirroring of preexisting hierarchies. Acting at a moment of crisis, Lincoln enacted a *refounding* moment.

REFOUNDING

In her discussion of a *virtuoso* politics, Bonnie Honig describes Hannah Arendt's "commitment to a non-foundational politics of (re) founding," a commitment that is also "an activist, democratic politics of contest, resistance, and amendment."[29] Emulation has its roots in the Homeric agon that is Honig's model of *virtú*. Indeed, the archetype of a mimetic culture is the picture of Hellenic Greece popularized by Werner Jaeger and Eric Havelock.[30] In their version of the fifth century, art—specifically agonistic recitals of the tales of the Trojan War—provides a framework for the transmission of virtues and traditions. Citizens engage in intense patterns of imitation and thus transmit the civic culture of their civilization. Although the story is known to all, the script is not permanently fixed— *The Iliad* and *The Odyssey* are, after all, only the most famous written versions of the tale, and the open competition of citizens to tell and retell the stories of their own virtue becomes a model for a spontaneous public action in politics and war as well as in the agora. The picture Wills draws of Lincoln is comparable to this vision of civic action: the Gettysburg Address is a way to carve out a new telling of the founding of the American Republic, a version that can save the United States from dissolution and prepare it for its re-creation as a centralized organic nation.

In Los Angeles, however, refounding is used to reify the hierarchies of city and state and to form a stage from which to mobilize private and public resources in *opposition* to the democratic politics of "contest, resistance, and amendment." In part this process has happened through the employment of mimesis. The elites of Los Angeles have been either involved directly in the mass media (newspaper editors, film and television producers) or adept at their use; the mass production of media in Los Angeles has provided the resources for an enormous mimetic project. By being able to claim that "this," this picture, this vision, "*is* the city," the authorized and legitimate picture of public life in Southern California, these elites have been able to fix the ground of politics. Civic contest has been defined by the mimetic promise of the *Los Angeles Times,* the major film studios, and television; attempts at political organization around counteridentities (African American, Mexican, organized labor, to name a few) have all begun at a disadvantage. The mimetic certainty that the defining virtues of Los Angeles have already been named has defined any external political contestation, in short, as resistance—and, generally, as illegitimate resistance.

What are those defining virtues? Los Angeles was founded by a small racially and socially heterogeneous group in the context of the Spanish empire, yet later Angeleno elites did not turn to this "original goodness" for protection from corruption. Rather than taking Los Angeles back to its moment of "founding excellence," in Machiavellian fashion, the first prominent Anglo elite enacted a refounding moment. Harrison Gray Otis, real estate baron and first publisher of the *Times,* defined Southern California as a peculiarly American paradise, a natural home for a population of spontaneous and inartificial heroes, a city of self-made men. Otis promised to clear away the structures of slavery in the westernmost part of the American continent and then create a community of entrepreneurial citizens, a political sphere structured by the imitation of radical innovators like himself. Thus Otis refounded Los Angeles as an American, not a Spanish, city.

The publisher promised to accomplish this, in part, through a process of emulation. The citizens worthy to rule in Los Angeles would be those who could successfully imitate and even exceed his own model; Otis's son-in-law, Harry Chandler, was one such exemplar. But even as a simple matter of definition, one cannot imitate radical innovation, and the task Otis demanded as a condition for political action proved more difficult than semantics would suggest. The monopolization of land, capital, advertising, information, and transportation was the foundation of his political and economic power; by the 1920s, Otis and his small circle created an elite that could not be imitated, much less emulated.

That did not contradict goals of the Otis/Chandler family, however. The publisher's primary means of mobilizing the population was not merely imitation; it was a brand of coercive mimesis forced on subject populations. War, in short, was Otis's primary model for the creation of political membership. "Liberty is the privilege of maturity," Woodrow Wilson wrote in the aftermath of the Spanish-American War, "of self-control, of mastery." The United States had wrested colonies away from the Spanish, and now democratic responsibility required that the American forces remain in place to provide the colonists an education, paradoxically, in self-governance. The occupied Filipinos "are children and we are men in these great matters of government and justice"; as American revolutionaries offered their emulatory struggle with great Romans to the former subjects of British North America, American soldiers would provide models of democracy to their subjects in the Pacific.[31] Emulation does not happen in colonies, however; subject populations with models thrust upon them are quite different from citizens engaging with exempla of their own choosing.[32] We have seen the paradox created when one is called to imitate radical innovation perfectly; when that paradox is placed at the gate to public life, when a nation's elites define that paradoxical mimesis as the defining goodness of the republic and the necessary path away from its corruption, it becomes devastating to the spontaneous creation of political alternatives and active diversity. In colonies, this paradox is more explicit, and more damaging.

"It is out of season to question at this time of day, the original policy of a conferring on every colony of the British Empire a mimic representation of the British Constitution," opined Sir Edward Cust in his 1839 report on West Africa to the British Colonial Office. "A fundamental principle appears to have been forgotten or overlooked in our system of colonial policy—that of colonial dependence. To give to a colony the forms of independence is a mockery; she would not be a colony for a single hour if she could maintain an independent station."[33] To demand mimetic faithfulness of a subject population is to demand political loyalty as well, and serves to strengthen the political hierarchies that produce it. The subject population may mimic Lucius Junius Brutus or George Washington, but they cannot *emulate* those models without fighting their own wars of independence. The presence of imperial troops, however, is intended precisely to prevent such a path. Also, and perhaps more important, donning the personae of one's conqueror carries its own price to a cultural movement for independence. The democratic pedagogy of colonialism is *designed* to create a lesser subject population, one that is located within the larger narrative of the imperial republic itself.

Harrison Gray Otis served in the Philippines; he commanded troops that put down revolutionary uprisings after the defeat of the Spanish. He put the lessons of his colonial war to work on a domestic population; Otis brought the mimesis of empire home to Los Angeles. From the 1880s into the 1960s, the *Los Angeles Times* reported the city imagined and refounded by Otis. In his revolution, a small circle of emulable capitalists fight a war to free California from the threat of slavery to an organized working class. The publisher and his allies mobilized huge resources of money, influence, and sheer coercion to defeat organized political opposition; working-class politics was, for the *Times,* an unauthorized and illegitimate invasion of Los Angeles public spaces. The battle for the city that became known within organized labor circles as "Otistown" was prolonged and extremely bloody; Otis was willing to fight a literal war to refound a Southern California village as an open-shop metropolis, and when he eventually achieved his victory, he began to teach the lessons Wilson wanted to impose on the Filipinos. Once a few emulable citizens had been welcomed into Otis's elite, the rest of the population was offered two models: an imitative and subject population or the demonized enemy that marked the borders of political membership. Control of the media and of the Southern California infrastructure guaranteed that those in the Otis/Chandler circle could physically map the city they wished to refound; their mimetic depiction of the publisher's utopia prepared the path for a colonized city to follow.

In chapter 1, I explore the story of Harrison Gray Otis in detail. I begin with a brief history of alternate founding moments for Los Angeles and then turn to an examination of the exemplar that Americans used to confront the gap between imitation and innovation. The self-made man was the central public model of American political thought in the nineteenth century; it both suggested an emulatory alternative to the Whig generation's dependence on European civic ideals and provided a rationale for narrow and coercive social and economic hierarchies. From that history I turn to Otis himself, whose biography spanned the Civil War, the Spanish-American War, and the refounding of Los Angeles in the fires of the war for Otistown. The *Times* publisher used the promise of self-making—that anyone could create an individual identity and destiny, and thus could scale the heights of political and economic influence if he or she so desired—as a rationale for excluding huge numbers of Angelenos from public life. The models he scripted were imposed on the population of the Southland, I argue, through a mimetic project developed as part of what Homi K. Bhabha refers to as "colonial mimesis."[34] The result was a military assault on the pluralistic public space that active republican politics requires.

Otis created an exclusionary hierarchy in the name of autonomy and self-determination and maintained it through economic monopoly and armed intervention. During the upheaval of the 1930s, however, labor unions and grassroots political mobilization returned to Southern California. Again large media companies led the way in defending L.A.'s rigid social and economic hierarchies, but during the Depression the newspapers were joined by a powerful new force in the Southland: the film industry. Major movie studios fought to control the content of American public spaces, in the actual politics of California and in the content of their films. In chapter 2, I turn to an examination of the politics and the film content at two major Hollywood studios, Metro-Goldwyn-Mayer and Warner Brothers. The production chiefs at MGM and Warner Brothers responded to the crises of the Depression by, they argued, mimetically reproducing the defining virtues of the American Republic. At MGM, Louis B. Mayer depicted a nation suffused with unrealized small-town excellence and promised audiences that they could be virtuous exempla with no more effort than that required to look into a mirror; in Southern California, meanwhile, Mayer worked harder than any of the studio heads to support and reinforce the open-shop structures created during the Otis-town war. Jack and Harry Warner, meanwhile, pledged their support to the Roosevelt administration and created a series of relatively low-budget films that depicted a fast-moving and dangerous urban America. Despite the Warners' support of New Deal politics, the studio's films depicted a stratified capitalist order that, Harry Warner promised, was merely a reflection of the "world as it is."[35]

During the massive mobilization of World War II, the Hollywood studios were forced to adapt their prewar genres, but not in ways that suggested radical alternatives or even counterappeals to the founding virtues of the American Republic. The studio chiefs worked in partnership with a variety of political actors at this time—the Popular Front years of the early 1940s saw successful coalitions of conservative Democrats, New Dealers, Socialists, and Communists—but they did so in the service of state mobilization and global warfare. After 1945, the new set of Southern California media elites made their peace with the newly expanded American security state, and the first concerted action of the postwar era was the dismantling of left-wing mobilization in Los Angeles. The House Un-American Activities Committee restructured the public spaces of Southern California and created the pretext for the arrest and blacklisting of liberal and radical Hollywood. More than that, HUAC's intervention into the film capital put the weight of the increasingly powerful national government behind the demands for colonial mimesis and the provision of narrow and strictly dictated narratives for all public actors. A brief period of crisis and wartime mobilization had created the context for different readings of American exempla and a broader group of "authorized" political actors in Southern California; by 1950, those alternatives had been coercively shut out of public life.

In chapter 3, I present an analysis of the career and legacy of Chief William Parker of the Los Angeles Police Department. Parker argued that American efforts to combat crime had been beset by a narrowness of vision, a blindness to the corruption that lay at the root of antisocial behavior. Crime, in Parker's analysis, was an outward symptom of precisely the sort of corruption that concerned Machiavelli; Americans, in the chief's words, were "disappointing Washington and the other founders . . . [b]y disassociating Virtue from our search for prosperity."[36] Only a mobilized mimetic commitment could rescue the nation from decay. Fortunately, the nation turned for much of its news and entertainment to Southern California; the chief was determined to make Los Angeles into a catalyst for the redemption of the United States. His LAPD would provide living pedagogical models, exempla of civic virtue; provided that Angelenos could follow in the footsteps of the police, the city and the nation would be rescued.

Some of Parker's language was explicitly emulatory. For his plan to work Angelenos would need to compete openly with their models of virtue; no police force was so virtuous that it could avoid corruption in a corrupted city. The form of Parker's vision, however, is hard to distinguish from that of Otis or the studio chiefs. Utterly mimetic media were to be the LAPD's primary tool in rescuing the nation from decay; the exact representation of Parker's ideals would provide the script for citizens to follow. In part, Parker did this through the cultivation of local media elites, but the LAPD also became involved in media production. Their signal success was Jack

Webb's highly rated *Dragnet,* a television show that promised to fix the identity of Los Angeles. Webb's show, produced under the direction of Parker's office, was intended to directly reproduce the chief's vision.

"This is the city. Los Angeles, California." With this statement of total ontological certainty, Webb defined the virtues, vices, and challenges of citizens in Los Angeles. The show presented citizens with a choice: to follow in the footsteps of its regimented protagonist or to succumb to the forces that continually threatened the peace, not through crime per se but through the erosion of virtue. For citizens who could not or would not match that model, Parker had other alternatives. Like Otis before him, Parker crafted a vision of politics in the service of colonial pedagogy. The chief's experience policing postwar Germany provided him with a vision of public life that was based less on emulatory civic struggle than on the demands of mimetic obedience. Some citizens might be able to match the models of the LAPD; primarily Parker turned to the white middle class—the PTA, the Rotarians, the Chamber of Commerce, the readership of the *Times,* and the Angelenos who could afford televisions in the 1950s—for this group. Others, particularly racial minorities, would need to be educated and contained, preserved by the force as a supportive population that had no appropriate autonomous role to play in the public world.

The Watts uprising of 1965 proved to Parker that his subject population could not be safely subjugated and that the white middle class could not be counted on for emulable virtue. That lesson served as the foundation of LAPD culture for another three decades as a series of Parker's students on the force explicitly policed Los Angeles as if it were a colonial possession. When, in 1992, Chief Daryl Gates refused to move his police force against the uprising in South-Central, it was because of this tenet of the LAPD philosophy: Los Angeles was "a foreign territory," in his words, "like Beirut" or "Kuwait," and the white middle class was composed of "civilians" and "traitors" who were not worth fighting for.[37] The vision of Southern California on which LAPD policy is premised is one that demands civic order, a narrow and structured public arena, and a privatized population. Gates's Los Angeles was not a political place where citizens compete with or emulate each other to achieve civic excellence. It was a city with no civic existence at all, where residents hide in their homes while their finest individuals venture into secret places to battle an opposing army.[38] If the occupied residents did enter the public world, Gates offered them a suitable model to imitate: LAPD officers at community watch meetings showed citizens how to behave while under arrest.

Gates's adoption of the viewpoint of an occupying army vis-à-vis the city he policed is radical in degree, but not in kind. The civic elites of Los Angeles discussed in this volume have all demanded—as many political actors in the history of the Republic have done—that the ideal citizen be spontaneous and studied, natural and artificial, perfectly mimicking models of founding innovation. Those who will not perform this impossible task (or who cannot because of ideological, racial, economic, and gendered policies of exclusion) are not augmenting the defining virtues of the nation and therefore are not legitimate occupants of the political world. As such, they are available for a different sort of mimetic training—not emulatory striving, but the simple mimicry of a subject population. This pattern is hardly unique to Los Angeles; it is my hope that mapping the centrality of the imitative project to political education in the California Southland will enable examinations of the exclusionary and colonial impulses at work in pedagogical strains of American democratic theory.

The attempt to use imitation to create and spread republican virtue has not been the only form of politics in Los Angeles, despite its centrality to many of Southern California's leading citizens. Indeed, an interest-based material politics has been more common. In chapter 4, I briefly consider a leading proponent of a nonimitative politics: Tom Bradley. Bradley was a successful mayor, providing resources and leadership for his constituents in general and his supporting coalition in particular. He was even capable of restraining LAPD influence on city politics. He was not capable, however, of redressing the most severe problems wrought by a decades-old legacy of political imitation. The exempla of successive attempts at mimetic virtue continue to affect policies in Southern California; merely retreating to bureaucratic or client-oriented politics as Bradley did is not sufficient to redress the legacy of Otis, HUAC, Gates, and the tradition of which they are a part. Similarly, the dystopian histories of Los Angeles that I discuss in chapter 4—reactionary classics such as director Ridley Scott's *Blade Runner* and Marxian critiques such as Mike Davis's eloquently persuasive *City of Quartz*—have been structured through the reassuring narrative of Southern California's fall from grace. As Honig notes:

The uncertainties of socio-economic, political and cultural change are borne more easily as part of the story of a Fall. The narrative consoles. The only problem is that all events and all subjects must conform henceforth to the narrative lest it be destabilized.[39]

The difficult task facing the scholar or the resident of Los Angeles is finding a way out of the narratives created by the city's refounding authorities, not merely retelling those stories as nightmare.

The political culture of Southern California is structured by more than a century's worth of attempts to exhort citizens to emulate models of political virtue and to coerce citizens to imitate models of quiescence. The political traditions of Los Angeles have been scripted in successive attempts to create a mimetic utopia. It is my plan to trace out this process in this book, and to theorize the traditions of democratic pedagogy and popular media that have been central to that utopian vision. Jack Webb's Los Angeles is, indeed, "the city," but it is not the only one.

chapter 1

A CITY OF SELF-MADE MEN

Harrison Gray Otis and Political Imitation in Los Angeles

> But the imitation of character as a means to autonomy is inherently
> paradoxical; it means copying those who copy no one. It implies both same-
> ness and radical difference between model and imitator. . . . The imitation of
> radical difference cannot result in the mutuality that practical, human,
> political autonomy requires.
>
> —HANNA PITKIN

In revolutionary American ideology, the emulation of exemplary public figures is a vital mechanism for the creation of a virtuous citizenry, providing both an agonal space for public action and an education in politics. Through the exempla of founders, in particular, American citizens would be capable of sustaining legitimate political struggle, authorized by the original actions of the first citizens. In fact, this process has been problematic; American citizens have been torn between the invocation of authorized struggle and the dread that any struggle against founders was impossible and even treasonous. In the public life of Los Angeles, this tension has erupted more than once in the course of more than a hundred years of civic struggle. The provision of exempla has been used as a tool for the suppression of spontaneous, grassroots political action; civic elites have coerced local populations, using exemplary models in attempts to script public life, supplanting the call to agonal and *virtuoso* action with imperialist demands for mimicry. The author of this process was Harrison Gray Otis, first publisher of the *Los Angeles Times*, who used his experience battling colonial subjects in the Philippines as a model for the political education he imposed on Los Angeles citizens. Otis's wars—the American Civil War, the Spanish-American War, and his own fourteen-year battle against organized labor—are the authorizing moment of modern Los Angeles, the substance of the city's refounding as an American metropolis.

The vision of Los Angeles as a utopia was premised on the timely invocation of the most popular American exemplar of the nineteenth century. The self-made man, who innovates even as he imitates others, was a favored model of public life in the United States, and Los Angeles elites at the turn of the twentieth century employed this model in an attempt to found a city of exemplary civic virtue.

Initially, however, the city's primary public model was a nostalgic and imperialist one. The Californios, the last generation of Mexican political elites in California, had represented themselves as radical innovators, moving away from Alta California's roots as part of a European empire. In the aftermath of the war with the United States, however, the Californios began to recall a very different history. Old California, as they described it in the memoirs and autobiographies known as the *testimonios,* was an Edenic place, characterized by an organic and stable hierarchy of aristocratic soldiers, benevolent friars, and simple, hardworking Indians. In this version of Southern California history, advancing Americans played the villains, but American audiences found the story compelling nevertheless.

Homi Bhabha's essay "Of Mimicry and Man: The Ambivalence of Colonial Discourse" casts an informative light on the progress of emulation and mimicry in the imperialist history of Southern California. Citing the imported culture of European colonies, Bhabha argues that imperialist nations attempted to inculcate the mimicry of deliberately inferior models of their culture rather than the competitive emulation of potentially threatening models of power and autonomy. Thus Alta California was created as a "New Spain," a territorial possession peopled by groups that could mimic the homeland—subjects, in Bhabha's words, "of a difference that is almost the same, but not quite."[1] After Mexican independence, the Californio elites rejected this categorization; if they resembled anyone, they argued, it was the revolutionary elites of the United States, not Spanish aristocrats. But their defeat in the war with the United States drove the Californios back to the subject position of the colonial mimic, leaving them as impoverished advocates of an idyllic and organic New Spain, a country rendered peaceful and whole through its connections with an imperialist and militarized aristocracy.[2] This vision of mimicry and military hierarchy was adapted for Los Angeles' refounding moment; the new "original excellence" of Southern California attempted to mimic this mimetic vision of Spanish virtue. The vision of the Californios, and of their popularizer in American letters, Helen Hunt Jackson, was compelling to American elites of the 1880s and 1890s.[3] The depiction of a society governed by an aristocratic class of soldiers pleased a group of landowners eager to represent themselves as members of an advancing imperial force while hoping to stave off comparisons with the land- and gold-hungry Yankee population that had moved to the Pacific Coast since the Civil War.

Thus the American "refounding" of Los Angeles did not completely break with this concept of Southern California's pre-U.S. history, but adapted it extensively, retaining a commitment to imperial hierarchy and mimesis while adding a republican rhetoric of self-making and emulatory virtue. Harrison Gray Otis, the man most responsible for the imagining and selling of an American city in Southern California, adopted a civic ideal that was militaristic, insisting that his allies refer to him as "General" and employing the imperial methods he learned in the Spanish-American War, transplanting his arena of action to the Southland from the Philippines. But despite these martial conceits, Otis preferred to cast himself in a different role. Rather than privileging the soldier-statesman persona more common for founding moments (as we saw in the case of the Roman-influenced American Revolutionaries), Otis cast himself as the Founder-as-Self-Made-Man. Otis insisted that the civic order in Los Angeles would be maintained through a strict division between emulable and armed self-made men and a growing subject population. The model Otis crafted would continue to regiment Southern California and to undermine its political life for decades.

In order to understand Los Angeles, we must briefly reexamine the exemplar that was invoked at the city's refounding. "Uncertain of the motives of others and worried about their own, Americans were preoccupied with natural states," writes Michael Rogin. "They glorified the authentic, spontaneous natural man who wore no masks, played no roles, and never dissembled."[4] Thus the "natural man" became a popular role to play, one that had to appear unstudied and that one was supposed to internalize. The American in the role of the "natural man" would deny the fact of his performance and, proffering the role of an actor who was sincere, spontaneous, and virtuous, would use imitation to break with the past rather than mimetically preserve it. Nineteenth-century Americans were wary of the open artifice and deferent position of an individual who claimed to imitate Washington or Jefferson (as well as the individual who might emulate such heroes). Republican citizens were supposed to be sincere and spontaneous actors, not mimics.[5] This immediately opened a gap, however, between a political exemplar and the narratives it authorized and that were used to maintain it. It is one thing to conserve and extend the political models of a society that premises legitimacy on the augmentation of an original and defining virtue, but how does one coherently connect a political education premised on innovation with the desire to imitate? How does a political actor simultaneously, as Machiavelli put it, walk always in the footsteps of others *and* tread new paths? The imperialist subjects in Bhabha's analysis resolve this problem by proffering different models for different actors; the imitators are never quite the same, especially when their exempla are models of obedience. Nineteenth-century Americans, however, promised that capitalist self-making provided a more egalitarian answer: the self-made man provided individuals with a model they could imitate while retaining the characteristics of spontaneous and ambitious innovation that Americans were supposed to prize.

Henry Clay first coined the term "self-made man" on February 2, 1832, in a defense of tariffs;[6] within twenty years, the self-made man was ubiquitous as an emulatory model.[7] The concept was more complex than the one with which we are familiar today. The aggregation of wealth by a young man of no familial connections and a personal history of poverty was central to the model, but this was not its sole defining feature. The nineteenth-century model of the self-made man was also characterized by a strong connection to the rest of society, a mature sense of autonomy, and the active sense of serving as a model to the young. By being a self-made man, one could engage in and help to transmit and preserve the principles of republican economic virtue.[8]

The self-made man was so popular that former exempla were recast in his mold; George Washington, who held himself up as a modern Cincinnatus, was depicted by Mason Weems and others as a "poor young man" whose "inheritance was but a small tract of poor land in Stafford county, and a few negroes" and who became a successful farmer and soldier through unceasing labor.[9]

Epitomized by Weems's biographies and such works as the McGuffey Readers and new editions of Benjamin Franklin's *Autobiography*, literary exhortations to self-making became a significant cultural cottage industry. By the 1850s, scores of collections of brief biographical sketches of self-made men were available, and William Makepeace Thayer was not alone in his contention that "the biography of every man who has risen to eminence of any kind by his own talent and industry is a lesson and stimulus to all who read it."[10] Thayer stressed the use of these biographies as a "stimulus" for emulatory purposes; the citizen who strove to be a truly *self*-made man would, paradoxically, have to do so in the footsteps of illustrious models, actively striving to best those exempla at their own game. Many of the authors who contributed to the plethora of self-made-man literature argued that their examples could aid in the creation of an active, autonomous, and virtuous population.[11] Such emulatory striving, the authors contended, would of itself benefit the Republic; by emulating models of the trailblazing and industrious, Americans would benefit the society as a whole, creating more employment, more wealth, and stronger moral character.

With the passage of time, the thesis that new men could effectively emulate earlier self-made men was widely questioned. Taking note of the growth of the trusts, self-made millionaires such as Andrew Carnegie warned that others would not be able to copy their achievements, much less surpass them, and Horatio Alger novels and popular guides for economic advancement began to eschew the moralizing biographical format in favor of self-help narratives that offered strategies for being a better employee. In short, some citizens would fail to emulate the exemplary self-made model, and could, therefore, strive to hold a supporting position in the nation's middle class of clerks, bureaucrats, and consumers. A growing class of laborers and immigrants, who, according to civic elites of both major political parties, had turned their backs on this privileged narrative of American public identity, occupied another, demonized, subordinate position, inhabiting the enemy role of unassimilable (if defining) Other. The refounding of Los Angeles combined different civic models and different populations, explicitly linking emulatory self-making with mimetic domestic imperialism. Harrison Gray Otis claimed this persona as his own.

Otis's political philosophy was an inherited blend of militant patriotism, Manichaean contrasts, and demands for autonomy (if not omnipotence). He was born in Marietta, Ohio, on February 10, 1837, the heir to a tradition of public life. Otis's grandfather Barnabas Otis served in the Revolutionary War from 1775 to 1776 on the Connecticut Line; the famous Revolutionary patriot James Otis was another ancestor, and namesake Harrison Gray Otis was an early Massachusetts senator.[12] Otis intended to live up to his family tradition of patriotism, but he looked to more contemporary models of good citizenship. His chosen model is apparent in the stories of his youth that he frequently told his grandchildren, the stories of earning and saving his first few pennies from digging potatoes and doing other related farmwork.[13]

Another important influence in Otis's early life was the abolitionist philosophy of his father, Stephen Otis. The Otis farm was a station on the Underground Railroad. In his truncated memoirs, Otis presents an early definition of proper American citizenship that combines a sense of historical tradition, a dedication to labor and to savings, and an opposition to the slave trade.[14] His later zeal in business matters was structured around images of slavery and autonomy: the self-made man was, for him, a warrior against enforced servitude. Paradoxically, however, this autonomy required strict political and economic hierarchy.

Emulating senior printers, the apprentice journalist Otis worked his way across the Midwest. In 1860, when he and his wife, Eliza, were living in Louisville, Kentucky, Otis journeyed to the Republican convention in Chicago as a state delegate and helped nominate Abraham Lincoln. Lincoln, "born in a lowly pioneer's cabin in the woods of Kentucky," was soon to inhabit the White House.[15] He opposed the extension of slavery to the new states of the West, "the places for poor people to go and better their condition."[16] Insofar as he opposed the spread of slavery and was popularly represented as a self-made man, Lincoln personified the central tenets of Otis's civic beliefs. Throughout his life, Otis would argue that the United States was in a conflict between the forces of freedom, personified by the self-made man, and the threat of slavery at the hands of all opponents of the emulatory struggle for wealth and power.

In 1861, Otis joined the Union Army and entered the Civil War as a private. Three years later, as a captain, he joined the Twenty-third Regiment of the Ohio Infantry, where he served under Rutherford B. Hayes and William McKinley. Warfare, with its strict hierarchies and violent imposition of civic tenets (the "civic religion" to which Lincoln referred in his Lyceum speech), was a model for the augmentation of the American founding as Otis saw it. Indeed, the Civil War was only the first of a series of armed conflicts to play a role in shaping Otis's view of virtuous political action. The young printer distinguished himself during the war, establishing a reputation as a hot-tempered but tireless fighter and winning the praise of Hayes. When he was discharged in 1865, Hayes's unsolicited recommendation won Otis a promotion to the rank of brevet colonel.[17]

After the war, Otis returned to Ohio and took over a small newspaper, but with his new Republican army connections, he quickly moved on to other things. With Hayes's help, he obtained a position in the U.S. Patent Office in Washington, D.C., and continued to foster his relationships with other members of the GOP. By the 1870s, Gottlieb and Wolt write in their outstanding history of the *Los Angeles Times,* Otis had "embraced the mainstream Republican ideology, an ideology which had gradually shifted from the radical libertarianism of the antislavery movement to the pro-business outlook of the large industrialists."[18]

In 1874, Otis and his family moved to California. It was on the far western frontier where Otis hoped to make his fortune, to vie as an exemplary citizen with the highest model of economic and political self-making, and to surpass that model. After a brief period in Santa Barbara, where his bombastic style of journalism had made him unpopular in polite society, Otis and his family settled in Los Angeles.[19] Otis took a job as editor of two advertising weeklies, the *Times* and the *Mirror,* in July 1882 and quickly attracted a coinvestor. Within four years, Otis bought out the other investor (H. H. Boyce, who went on to publish the *Los Angeles Tribune*) and became sole owner of a rapidly growing daily, the *Los Angeles Times.* On April 5, 1886, Otis editorialized that the mission of the "new" *Times* was the "maintenance of the principles of the Republican Party, the defense of liberty, law, and public morals, and the upbuilding of the city and county of Los Angeles and the *state of Southern California.* The motto of the now united proprietors will be, PUSH THINGS!"[20]

This editorial perfectly sums up the form in which Otis's self-made-man credo played out an essential role in the early growth of Los Angeles: the combination of belligerent patriotism, concern for public morality, and economic boosterism, personalized in the "united proprietors," who, despite the use of the plural, was Harrison Gray Otis himself. In a stream of articles, editorials, and letters, Otis would urge the citizens of Los Angeles to assert their "self-respecting manhood," to engage in a war against "bandits and plutocrats," "lawlessness," and "slavery" until they succeeded in creating a city that could serve the nation as a model of freedom, virtue, and economic success.[21] The publisher used his paper to teach the virtues necessary for his civic enterprise, urging his fellows to follow the model he was setting, daily, in the *Times*. In the rapidly expanding population of Southern California, he looked to find or to create the group of men who could serve as his apprentices and, eventually, as his fellow civic exempla for the Southland and the nation.

Los Angeles in 1886 was undergoing a boom in settlement. A rate war between the Southern Pacific and the Atchison, Topeka, and Santa Fe railroads drove the price of train tickets from the Midwest to record lows (in some cases as cheap as one dollar), and the village of Los Angeles became a city in a matter of months. Deed conveyances rose from 6,490 in 1885 to 34,000 in 1887; Los Angeles property, assessed at $7.6 million in 1881, had grown to $39.5 million in 1888. Towns in the area around L.A. were created in real estate booms, with lots sold before any building had begun. In 1880, Pomona did not exist; in 1889, it was a town with a population of more than five thousand.[22] It was in this hive of rapidly expanding real estate empires that Otis began the creation of his masterpiece.

The *Times* was the organ in which Otis developed his vision of an ideal American city. He would create a city with a "state of culture and philosophy such as prevailed along the shores of ancient Greece in her palmy days," resulting from "republican and industrial freedom," and in which citizens fairly competed for "honor, wealth, and power," acting in the fashion of men such as Lincoln, Davy Crockett, and Otis himself.[23] In Otis's ideal scenario, Los Angeles would be like the "free country" that Machiavelli describes in *Discourses,* in which "riches multiply . . . for each man gladly increases such things and seeks to gain such goods as he believes, when gained, he can enjoy. Thence it comes that men in emulation give thought to private and public advantages, and both kinds keep marvelously increasing."[24] Otis was determined that Los Angeles become a model of "industrial freedom" for the rest of the nation, a city where private advantage and public advantage would both be favored by the striving of self-made men with a model of the ideal citizen.

Otis provided a refounding moment for Los Angeles; the city was not, he insisted, a conquered holdover from a European empire, but an American center of self-making and republican autonomy. He centered his quest to create a city of self-made men through war won by the crafting of colonial personae. Subservient roles, inscribed within and below an Anglo political structure, could be mimicked on broad levels by increasing numbers of people, and aristocrats would emulate the "self-made" ideal of Otis's invention. Otis achieved the refounder's position, in short, by bringing colonialism home to California.

Otis's first formative battle was the American Civil War, in which, he argued, the Republican Party successfully imposed individualist capitalism on the formerly slaveholding states. Beaten foes must adopt the civic culture of the victors; ex-Confederates would need to learn how to mimic the vision of virtuous citizenship associated with the North. As Hanna Pitkin tells us, however, the command that a rescued inferior mimic his or her savior's innovative *virtù* creates a pattern of hierarchy and subjugation, not civic freedom. When the model of a public life imposed on the foe is a figure of self-made virtue, the affect is even more negative: to be an autonomous American citizen, the fallen rebel would need to be self-authorizing while simultaneously mimicking his or her conqueror. This double bind was imposed on a number of Otis's enemies: southern rebels, Filipino freedom fighters, and Southern California labor organizers. The pattern, however, is reflective of a larger contradiction at the heart of American political identity. Torn between the dictates of loyalty to the founding and reverence for revolutionary innovation, American citizens have lauded autonomous figures while insisting that they be copied. The self-made man, envisioned as a competitive and emulatory bridge over the gap between innovator and imitator, in fact only deepened it, as the model was imposed on citizens as a way to defeat radical and progressive organizations that, as collective civic bodies, were redefined as insufficiently individualistic.

Before moving to his second defining war, the Spanish-American, Otis needed to do battle at home with the premier capitalistic organization of California, the Southern Pacific Railroad. It is unsurprising that Otis's metropolis of individual capitalists would collide with the archetypal western monopoly, a fight, as Otis saw it, between genuine businessmen and "a group of bandits and plutocrats."[25] Since the 1780s, the closest thing the Los Angeles area had to a natural water port was the small San Pedro Bay, twenty miles south of the city. Indeed, "until the gold rush, San Pedro had been one of the most important shipping ports on the West Coast."[26] It was natural to think of San Pedro as the site of the harbor that Los Angeles would need to develop in order to be a major western city. The Southern Pacific and its president, Senator Leland Stanford, worked to develop the site, and real estate interests in the city formed the Los Angeles Terminal Railway Corporation to develop tramlines from the city proper to the harbor area. In 1890, the U.S. Congress authorized a survey by the U.S. Army Corps of Engineers of potential harbor sites for Los Angeles, and San Pedro was chosen as the best location. Also in 1890, however, Colis P. Huntington replaced Leland Stanford as president of the Southern Pacific, and advocated the building of a port at Santa Monica, where the railroad held a monopoly on real estate and rail access. In response to an outcry from the budding tram and real estate entrepreneurs of the new city, Huntington offered money and influence in Congress for a Santa Monica harbor and opposition to a port in San Pedro.

Otis was outraged. As the harbor funding issue entered debate in the U.S. Senate (where Huntington confidant William Pierce Frye chaired the hearings in the Rivers and Harbors Committee), the *Times* editorial page thundered out adjurations to the "self-respecting manhood" of the entrepreneurial middle-class citizens of Los Angeles.[27] By the mid-1890s, the *Times* had formed the Free Harbor League and combined local advocacy and rallies with intensified lobbying in Washington. After nine years, three additional surveys by the Army Corps of Engineers, several heated committee battles, and *Times* charges that Senator Frye was corrupt, the battle for a "free" harbor (i.e., one not surrounded by Southern Pacific holdings in land and rail) in San Pedro was won. The huge bronze American eagle on top of the *Times* building was installed with a powerful whistle, which trumpeted the league's victory, and a large crowd of people marched to the building to celebrate.

Otis, however, was not at the *Times* to join in the celebration. The publisher had moved back into the arena of national affairs, mobilized as part of the conflict in which the United States acquired its first explicit colonial holdings. Without losing interest in the free harbor battle, Otis had become fixated on the idea of returning to the martial activities of his youth, and he pestered his Republican connections in Washington for a command in the Spanish-American War. By the time he was commissioned, however, the war was over. Otis was assigned to help consolidate the U.S. position in the Philippines. Shortly after he arrived there, the Filipinos rose up against the U.S. forces, and Otis worked sixteen-hour days in a campaign to defeat the local soldiery. His brigade led several charges, engaged in a four-day battle at La Loma, and participated in the capture of Malalos. In July 1899, Otis returned to Los Angeles a war hero, decorated and promoted to brevet major general of volunteers.[28]

His letters reveal a mixture of hostility and paternalistic contempt toward the Filipinos. Although Otis was incensed at the Filipino "insurrection," he chiefly argued that the "enemy" in the Pacific was more benighted than malicious, and he perceived his primary mission to be the extension of American republicanism to a backward population.[29] Bhabha argues that "colonial mimicry is the desire for a reformed, recognizable Other, as a subject of difference that is almost the same, but not quite."[30] In his second war, Otis constructed a model for a "reformed and recognizable" Other in America's new colonial possessions. He continued to employ this exemplar, a model crafted for a subjugated population incapable of emulation, when he returned to Los Angeles. Otis treated the majority of the members of Los Angeles' middle class with a contempt similar to his attitude toward the Filipinos because none of them seemed capable of or willing to strive with the model that he set forth. The majority of California residents—Mexican and Chinese immigrants, members of the working class, and middle class citizens—were, in Otis's view, as benighted as the native armies he fought in the Pacific. For citizens so lacking in ambition, Otis proffered the quiescent model of the foot soldier. The increasingly confined civic life of the California Southland is not the result of a failed attempt at emulation; rather, it illustrates specific problems with the popular self-made-man model and within the practice of political imitation itself.

Before I turn to the few citizens Otis deemed worthy of the emulatory challenge, I need to address the battle that the publisher saw as his most important struggle: the war for the "open shop." During the unstable "boom and bust" period of the 1880s, Otis had engaged in a few skirmishes with local unions, but nothing of great significance. Indeed, he was quick to remind his union printers that in his youth he had belonged to a typographers' union. Nonetheless, he recognized the economic realities of Los Angeles' situation. San Francisco, with its natural harbor, large manufacturing base, access to nearby farmland and mining areas, and large amounts of capital built up during the gold rush, held an enormous lead as the civic and manufacturing base of the American West. Otis's dreams of empire required that Los Angeles be a more attractive industrial base than the Bay Area; the central economic position of San Francisco could preclude the growth of Los Angeles to the level that Otis had set for it. One requirement, of course, was the creation of a substantial harbor. Having settled that issue, the publisher turned to a new stratagem: undercutting San Francisco's wage structure.[31]

San Francisco had been unionized for many years by the time Otis arrived in Los Angeles. The only economic advantages that L.A. had during the 1880s were the booming real estate market and the enormous amount of land at the city's disposal. Otis worked to forge an economic rival to San Francisco, wooing large numbers of workers to the Southland, encouraging their quick establishment of equity in private homes, and fighting to keep large-scale unions out of Southern California. In doing so, he argued, he was carrying out an important task of republican virtue: creating an open shop in his city meant "standing for the right of every man to be a man, and against the infamy of making any man or body of men in America industrial slaves," the same good fight for a virtuous self-made citizenry that he had been fighting since the Civil War.[32] As Carey McWilliams demonstrates, the economics of Los Angeles made the fight for the open shop seem inevitable, but the degree to which it was nationally personalized as General Otis's war (indeed, by the height of the fighting, from 1907 to 1911, union members from all over the United States referred to Los Angeles as Otistown) and the bloodiness of that war were set by the publisher's zealotry.[33]

Otis made his first incursions onto enemy territory in 1890, the same year he began his battle with the railroads. During a bust period in the local economy, Otis formed the Newspaper Publishers' Union with the publishers of the major Los Angeles dailies and made a deal with the Printers Protective Fraternity of Kansas City to provide strikebreakers before presenting the powerful Los Angeles Typographical Union with a cut in pay and a lockout. Otis failed to hold his allies in line, however; the other publishers quickly arrived at settlements with the LATU.[34]

In the end, Otis arrived at a settlement with the union. From the union's perspective, the victory cost the *Times* little: Otis maintained control over wages and hours, settled all worker grievances on a case-by-case basis, did not have to fire the strikebreakers from Kansas City, and only agreed to hire four union employees he had fired early in the strike. But he had recognized the union, a victory for organized labor that Otis chalked up to the lack of a strong supporting organization of his own.

Otis, in Gottlieb and Wolt's words, "saw the conflict in military terms . . . a full-fledged crusade to banish the entire Los Angeles labor movement."[35] The General's forces were too dispersed, too susceptible to cowardice and treachery, for the war to end successfully. The autonomous condition of a city of self-made men required, Otis argued, a degree of moral courage that he feared most members of the Angeleno middle class did not possess. The publisher thus drew a sharp division between those who could emulate his example and those who must adopt other, lesser models: the city population would be composed of an aristocratic elite, a subjugated population, and a supportive middle class that was similar to the exemplar created by Otis, but "not quite."

The publisher set his sights on creating an organization that could hold the wavering middle class in line until the city was safe from "industrial slavery." In his future battles, he would act at the head of an organization that could enforce military-style discipline over the entrepreneurs of the California Southland.[36] This organization was the Merchants and Manufacturers' Association.[37] Created in 1896 as a booster and advertising organization (the M&M, as it was called, sponsored such events as La Fiesta de las Flores and the Los Angeles International Air Meet),[38] the M&M under Otis's leadership became the nation's leading proponent of the open shop. In 1901, the International Typographers Union and the American Federation of Labor struck the *Times,* using parades, public education campaigns, and boycotts, offering pedagogical and political alternatives to Otis's model of civic participation. For Otis, this was a declaration of war, and the resulting bloody conflict would last ten years. As Gottlieb and Wolt note, "The M&M entry into the Los Angeles struggle marked the beginning of one of the most ruthless and systematic campaigns against organized labor in the history of the United States."[39]

Of the city's major firms, 80 percent subscribed to the boostering organization, and M&M president Felix Zeehandelaar and Otis put the subscription list to work, raising an initial sum of $25,000 to hire strikebreakers and scab labor. Other sums of money were raised to hire security guards and police protection. Indeed, the Los Angeles Police Department became closely affiliated with the M&M through its willingness to deputize M&M strikebreakers.[40] The *Times* ran an educational campaign of its own, decrying the evils of unionism and defining civic duty as loyalty to employers.

Otis had not abandoned the ideal of the self-made citizen, and he was not worried about the few individuals who would follow his path through their own ambition. He welcomed the small number of civic actors who could successfully ascend the economic hierarchy to elite status; such emulatory heroes could be trusted to maintain the exemplary city he was attempting to found. He needed to maintain the loyalty of the turncoat business community, however, and that required M&M coercion of local entrepreneurs and middle-class citizens. With the cooperation of the vast majority of the Los Angeles business community, the M&M could withhold bank loans and supplies, delay payments, and cancel newspaper advertising for recalcitrant business owners, as well as boycott employers who were willing to negotiate with the unions. In the words of Frederick Palmer in the January 1911 issue of *Hampton's Magazine,* the M&M was "without rival in its effective coherence. . . . Always alert is Otis with his daily newspaper ready to beat any laggard into line. It is not popular and it is not wise for a businessman to get in bad with 'M and M.'"[41] In Otis's words:

> We are against the weak-kneed employer who, at the first sign of danger, surrenders his position to the assaults of lawless labor, in whatever guise it may come, and who fails to assert his indefeasible rights under the law to manage his business in his own way.[42]

That "way" was Otis's way. After years of equating "manliness" and autonomy with economic self-making, Otis now identified such virtues with the willingness to follow his lead in the crusade against organized labor.[43]

As a nationally famous adherent of the open shop, Otis finally achieved the exemplary status he had been seeking. In 1903, the National Association of Manufacturers formed the Citizens' Industrial Association, devoted to the cause of the open shop and openly modeled on the actions of the M&M. Otis set out in 1886 to make Los Angeles a city of freedom, "culture," and "philosophy" like those of "ancient Greece" but populated by self-made men, good citizens who would strive with his example of economic and political virtue.[44] The model of Los Angeles that became widely influential, however, was a model of coercion and apolitical regimentation. This was not because Otis had strayed from the attempt to engage in political emulation; it reflected, rather, an inherent element of the model that he chose. The model of the self-made man required a paradoxical submission to outside authority. In Los Angeles, Otis recognized only a handful of emulatory citizens, and they were his allies. Any opposition—in other words, any political organization that was not premised on Republican models of individualism—was, in his civic language, a force for slavery, and the rest of the population had to choose sides in the conflict. In the *Times'* war, autonomy necessitated surrender, a public life dedicated to the imitation of an innovative exemplar that could not be matched. This vision of political life could not sustain a pluralistic civic arena; indeed, it was premised on opposition to any such space.

Otis, then, was engaged in an imperial war in the California Southland, as he had been in the Philippines. Woodrow Wilson, Senator Albert Beveridge, and other American elites had argued in the aftermath of the Spanish-American War that Filipinos, subject for previous decades to a Spanish monarch and lacking any intrinsic Anglo-Saxon capacity for self-governance, would need to be forcibly instructed in democracy until they could appropriately mimic the American victors. Now, "the General" brought the logic of imperial mimesis to bear on Los Angeles. Michael Rogin and Richard Slotkin have demonstrated the way that newspaper publishers and editors transposed the category of "red" Native Americans to "Red" labor activists in American cities in the latter half of the nineteenth century.[45] In a number of cities, elites thus offered populations with less economic and political power the choice of mimicking the persona of "self-made" employees or being accused of mimicking the demonized others that served to delineate America's borders. In Los Angeles, this process went further. Otis demanded a mimetic obedience from the other inhabitants of Southern California, even his own supporters within the M&M, if they proved incapable of self-making in his footsteps.

Indeed, Otis and the M&M faced formidable resistance, from labor unions and from much of the Angeleno public as well. According to Otis, Los Angeles by 1910 had become a national symbol of economic autonomy, possessor of "that priceless boon, industrial freedom."[46] Southland industry was growing rapidly, and the unionized city of San Francisco was beginning to lag behind. Bay Area employers put pressure on the local unions: either the companies in Southern California became organized, they warned, or workers in San Francisco would have to take large cuts in pay. Members of major Bay Area unions and of the American Federation of Labor went to Southern California to help prepare for the battle to eradicate the open shop in Los Angeles, "the scabbiest town on earth."[47] When the Los Angeles Brewery Owners and the metal trade employers' associations attacked the last two strong unions in the Southland, announcing they would not renew the union contracts, the last and bloodiest battles in Otis's war began.[48]

The M&M acted swiftly to maintain unity among the members of the L.A. business community while statewide labor organizations directed funds and personnel to Los Angeles. In July 1910, the L.A. City Council unanimously passed a ban on all picketing and "certain" public meetings at the urging of the M&M.[49] Workers maintained their strike and hundreds of arrests occurred, leading to fighting in the streets and in the jails. Otis responded with incendiary headlines ("Union Labor Breaks Bones"; "Not Enough Bloodshed Here for Labor Bosses") and a new barrage of editorials accusing the "foreign element" of union organizers of bloodthirsty plotting. Local support for the unions was strong, however, and local labor organizations planned a mass parade to open the State Labor Convention on October 3, 1910. But before the convention began, Otis and the M&M suffered an attack that would win their war for them.[50]

On October 3, at 1:07 A.M., the *Los Angeles Times* building was destroyed. An explosion on the first floor ignited tons of flammable ink, spreading an inferno through the building in moments. A hundred workers on the night shift were trapped in the flames, and twenty-one of them died. Otis published a one-page edition of the *Times* the following day from an emergency auxiliary plant, announcing that the "Crime of the

Century," "one of the worst atrocities in the history of the world," had been perpetrated by the unions. The cause of the blast was initially unclear, for *Times* employees had complained of gas fumes previously and on the night of the explosion, but Otis was certain that the explosion was not accidental.[51] When unexploded dynamite was subsequently discovered hidden at the homes of Otis and Zeehandelaar, the city business community was certain the case against organized labor had been settled.

Los Angeles Mayor George Alexander hired detective William Burns, who had recently gained fame for uncovering graft in the administration of San Francisco Mayor Abe Reuf, to find the individuals responsible for the bombing. Acting on the testimony of a suspect in another bombing case, Burns charged John J. McNamara, president of the militant International Association of Bridge and Structural Iron Workers' Union, and his

Disaster at the *Los Angeles Times,* October 10, 1910. Courtesy of California Historical Society, Title Insurance and Trust Photo Collection, and of University of Southern California, on behalf of the U.S.C. Specialized Libraries and Archival Collections, Department of Special Collections, U.S.C. 7500.

younger brother, James B. McNamara, with the bombing.[52] Burns arrested the McNamaras and sped them back to Los Angeles for trial.[53]

The case that Burns made was far from conclusive, and the labor community of Los Angeles argued that the McNamaras had been framed. Clarence Darrow agreed to defend the brothers. As one of his assistants Darrow hired Job Harriman, a Los Angeles attorney who had previously run for governor and U.S. vice president as a Socialist candidate. It was while he was on the McNamara defense team that Harriman announced his candidacy for mayor of Los Angeles.[54]

The combination of an attack on the *Times* and a viable Socialist mayoral candidate represented, according to Otis, the most serious crisis in the history of Los Angeles. "The ambivalence of mimicry," Bhabha observes, the "almost but not quite—suggests that the fetishized colonial culture is potentially and strategically an insurgent counter-appeal."[55] Labor unions, Socialists, and Progressive Republicans who saw the power of the M&M as an obstacle to the autonomy of American workers used Otis's language of political and economic autonomy against him, providing a counter-appeal to the revolutionary traditions of the Republic.

For years, Otis had openly fought the Progressive wing of the Republican Party, charging the Progressives with treasonous tendencies and a complete unwillingness to follow the tradition of which he saw himself as an exemplar. As a result of this division, the *Times* had never supported Alexander's Progressive Republican administration, and the divided loyalty of the Los Angeles GOP helped the Socialist candidate to quickly establish a lead in the polls. Harriman expanded his base of support by capitalizing on voter suspicion of the newly announced aqueduct to bring water from the Owens Valley. The *Herald-Examiner* had recently published a story establishing that the M&M, the *Times,* and Moses Sherman of the Los Angeles Water Commission had bought extensive real estate in the San Fernando Valley, where the aqueduct would lead and which was being incorporated into the city. The charge of corruption seemed viable, supported by the obvious conflicts of interest surrounding the aqueduct (for which two bonds had already been passed and still more civic funds were required) and the public concentration of power in the hands of Harrison Gray Otis.[56]

The M&M did little, in fact, to dispel the impression of such corruption. While Otis continued to combine incendiary speeches with daily trips around Los Angeles in a limousine with a cannon mounted on the roof, the City Council struck the names of twelve hundred registered voters (those living in lodging houses) from the rolls. All the newspapers in town imposed a blackout on Harriman's campaign. Secure in his public identity as an exemplar of self-made civic virtue, Otis found it impossible to imagine that many Angelenos could perceive him as corrupt, greedy, or bloodthirsty, or that the role of socialistic nemesis with which he branded them could become a rallying point against his elite position.

Harriman's attack on the aqueduct and his role in defending the McNamara brothers helped to increase his popularity. The case against the brothers was suspicious, and hundreds of sympathetic workers in the city wore "McNamaras Innocent! Vote for Harriman!" buttons while contributions to the McNamara Defense Fund poured in from all over the nation. Sharing the public spotlight with Clarence Darrow, Harriman provided a striking contrast to Mayor Alexander, who had ceased to give any interviews or make any public appearances. Convinced of the danger to their open-shop city, Los Angeles Republicans began to work together for the incumbent's campaign. Harriman's greatest threat, however, did not arise from Otis's model and the portion of Los Angeles that embraced it. The decisive blow against the Socialist campaign came from within.[57]

Darrow increasingly doubted the innocence of his clients and began to consider a pretrial arrangement a necessity. Without consulting with or even informing Harriman, the defense attorney commissioned muckraking journalist Lincoln Steffens to establish a compromise settlement with the civic leaders of Los Angeles. Confident that he and a nonpartisan group of the city's political and economic elite could forge a deal that would save the McNamaras from hanging and Otis from creating martyrs that could spell his undoing, Steffens approached leading figures in the M&M, including Otis's son-in-law, Harry Chandler. Chandler assured Steffens that a guilty plea would save the McNamaras' lives, result in a light sentence for John McNamara, and create an advantageous peace for employers and unions alike in Los Angeles. Chandler also promised that the posttrial period would begin with a labor-capital conference to settle the bloody strife between the two factions. Remarkably, Steffens took Chandler at his word. Also remarkably, Chandler convinced his father-in-law to support the deal, despite Otis's public cries for the McNamaras' blood. On December 1, 1911, four days before the mayoral election, Darrow changed the McNamaras' plea to guilty. Sentencing was set for election day. On December 5, with the union heroes discredited by the changed plea, George Alexander was reelected mayor, and the labor movement in Los Angeles lost tremendous support. The M&M was victorious.[58]

"The God that is still in Israel filled the souls of the dynamiters with a torment they could not bear," Otis crowed from the *Times* front page. "God's people spoke, and the enemies of God stand confused. Scoffing, anarchistic Socialism has been crushed—as far as this city is concerned—with the same swift merciless annihilation that the heel of a giant crushed the head of a reptile."[59] According to Otis, the 1911 election demonstrated the righteousness of his cause; Los Angeles was free to be a model of industrial autonomy, where the strong of spirit could emulate his model of economic, military, and political supremacy. Even "weak-kneed" citizens would do their duty, following the model of loyal soldiers in his war to create a model city of "economic liberty," a city where later generations could be wealthy and virtuous self-made men without fear of "industrial slavery."[60] By the end of his war for the open shop, Otis succeeded in imposing two imitative models on the population of Los Angeles: for some, a "self-made man" that was, in Bhabha's words, "a subject of difference that is almost the same, but not quite," and for others, the demonized figure of treasonous political opposition, organized groups that, by resisting the publisher's exemplar, announced their support for slavery and their disloyalty to the American nation. Despite the tank-limousines, the police dragnets, and other signs of megalomania and appearances of corruption, Otis stayed true to his armed-camp vision of emulatory civic virtue. He had created a new founding for a new Los Angeles, a city whose defining virtues combined the imperialist hierarchy of the city's Spanish "prehistory" with the autonomous rhetoric of nineteenth-century American self-making. Indeed, by the 1911 election, the General had already been preparing two apprentices to enter the civic world of self-made citizen leaders: William Mulholland and Harry Chandler.

Harry Chandler was born in New Hampshire in 1864 to a family of farmers. He had been attending Dartmouth College for less than a year when he leapt into a frozen vat of starch on a dare and almost immediately succumbed to pneumonia and a hemorrhage of the lungs. On doctors' advice, he moved to Southern California. He arrived in Los Angeles, ill and penniless, in 1883. After a brief stint picking and selling fruit in the

San Fernando Valley, Chandler accepted a job as a circulation clerk at the *Times* and, shortly after, started a newspaper circulation business of his own. Using savings from his fruit sales, Chandler obtained a monopoly on the circulation lists of the rival *Herald* as well as routes for the *Times,* and he used the two circulation lists to drive the *Tribune* out of business. He then purchased the *Tribune* plant, machinery, subscription lists, and circulation routes, and negotiated their sale to Otis. Otis hired him as circulation manager. Within two years, Chandler was married to his boss's daughter; within three, he was business manager of the *Times*.[61]

Chandler, a brilliant entrepreneur, seemed the very definition of a self-made man. Able to accumulate vast amounts of initial capital, the heir to the *Times* was a master at assembling commercial syndicates, drawing together oil, transportation, and real estate magnates with civic officials to create cities all over the California Southland. Once his real estate ventures were financed, Chandler trumpeted the area and the Southland in general, using the *Times,* his promotional organization (the All-Year Club), and national advertising to draw homesteaders to Los Angeles (creating both real estate revenue and a surplus of labor).[62] By the time of his death in 1941, Harry Chandler was one of the wealthiest men in the country.[63]

William Mulholland was able to match the rags-to-riches story of Chandler as well as the civic model of self-making originally proffered by Otis. Born in Dublin in 1855, Mulholland signed on to the crew of a merchant ship as an apprentice seaman at age fifteen. Soon after arriving in the United States, he was hired on a well-drilling rig in San Pedro; he later became a ditchdigger for the Los Angeles City Water Company. Fascinated by water, he spent hours wandering the banks of the Los Angeles River, studying its peculiarities and "dreaming of the ways he could fashion its uncertain flows to build a great city," determined to create a water system that would allow for the growth of a new metropolis.[64] Working tirelessly on a variety of projects for the Water Company, Mulholland attracted the attention of his superiors and rapidly ascended the company's hierarchy.

Mulholland worked on himself as he worked on the city's water system. With a visceral feeling for the nineteenth century's vision of the self-made man, he combined long hours at his job and the planning of a great new city with late nights of intensive reading. In William Kahrl's words, Mulholland's "passions in reading were those of a young man seeking to better himself," and to do this the young engineer sought out a knowledge

Portrait of William Mulholland. Courtesy of Herald-Examiner Collection,
Los Angeles Public Library 00043872.

of technical affairs and of great models of human nature.[65] "The only feasible way to study mankind is reading good books, written by men who were masters of their art," Mulholland commented. "Damn a man who doesn't read books. The test of a man is his knowledge of humanity, and of the politics of human life, his comprehension of the things that move men."[66] In his expanding role as one of the central figures of the founding period of Los Angeles, Mulholland consciously personified the nineteenth-century version of the self-made man, a public model of hard work and civic responsibility that competed with exempla from history and invited the scrutiny of the citizens for whom he worked.[67]

The construction of the Owens Valley Aqueduct would establish both men as master craftsmen worthy to share (if not quite surpass) Otis's exemplary position. It also, however, closed off the emulatory option for the vast majority of Angelenos in their own time and in the future. In February 1903, the city of Los Angeles took possession of the Los Angeles City Water Company, thereby securing municipal control of the city's water supply. At the same time, the city procured the services of Mulholland, the company's most promising engineer. Mulholland secured his reputation by repairing the slipshod water system that had been installed while the company was under private ownership. He also set to work trying to find alternative supplies of water for Los Angeles, whose desert climate was not appropriate to the large city beginning to take shape under the aegis of the *Times* and the M&M. Joseph Lippincott, a government engineer who moonlighted as an investigator of Southern California water sources for Los Angeles, joined Mulholland in these endeavors. Lippincott's primary job was engineering work for the Federal Reclamation Service, and, in that capacity he had been investigating the irrigation potential of the Owens Valley. Lippincott denied that his two jobs conflicted. He proceeded, however, to lobby against the uses of the valley for the Reclamation Service and apparently helped carry information between the L.A. Department of Water and Power and the voters of the Owens Valley. Mulholland conceived the plan for providing the Owens waters to Los Angeles. A proposal for a bond to raise money for an aqueduct soon appeared on a municipal ballot.[68]

By this point, Mulholland had grown sure of the importance of placing himself and his water plans squarely in the public eye, certain of the civic importance of his aqueduct and of his own example of citizenship. Otis, meanwhile, had taken a favorable interest in his fellow self-made man. As the aqueduct project dragged on in time and expense, and the chances for more successful bond issues grew dim, Mulholland began reporting exaggerated dangers of drought.[69] A severe drought, he argued, would mean an effective end to growth for the desert metropolis. The *Times* provided Mulholland with an outlet for his "dire predictions" alongside its own stories of a Los Angeles reclaimed by the desert. The paper also printed grandiose promises of the golden future the aqueduct could bring. Oddly enough, however, the paper dwelled more on the great progress in store for the unincorporated San Fernando Valley than it did on the benefits for the city itself. Mulholland was to serve as the sorcerer helping to secure a golden future for the pastoral area,[70] a golden future reminiscent of a biblical past: "The San Fernando Valley can be converted into a veritable Garden of Eden. Vast areas of land, devoted now to grazing and grain, will be converted into orchards and gardens, the peer of any in the world."[71]

And what divinity would create these gardens once Mulholland had slain the arid demon? A community of politically and economically motivated self-made men. The story was initially broken by Otis's rival, Hearst's *Herald-Examiner*, but Otis responded by turning the indictment into a boast:[72] The *Times* publisher and a number of other wealthy Angelenos had formed a syndicate, the masterwork of Harry Chandler, and were buying up large amounts of land in the San Fernando Valley. The *Times*' promise of a paradise on earth had already created a bullish real estate market in the valley, and the aqueduct would make a fortune for the members of the syndicate. For Otis, this was proof of his own exemplary status: combining a quick eye for profit with long-range civic vision, he was preparing to double the size of his metropolis. He had also, however, frozen the vast majority of Angelenos out of the ability to do likewise. As the economic and political elite of Los Angeles grew wealthier and in command of more real estate and influence, it became increasingly impossible for anyone to emulate Otis. Those who did join his elite, in fact, grew less concerned with civic matters, and Otis began to compare himself with even loftier models than Lincoln or Washington:

> Not since the days of Caesar and his Roman Aqueduct has the world recorded an engineering accomplishment aqueductorial equal to this gathering of the waters . . . [for] the salvation of the half a million souls which are now

and the added half million soon to be in the incomparable City of the Golden West. . . . a great river has been turned from its course—a course that it followed since the hand of God raised the mountains and laid the oceans in their place on the morn of creation—and brought down to serve the people of Los Angeles who are here today, and the millions more who are to come tomorrow, and tomorrow, and tomorrow.[73]

In this editorial we see clearly where Otis finds himself in the years before his death: his enemies vanquished, his city established, looking generations into the future, Otis portrays himself as one who had successfully surpassed even Abraham, a patriarch of innumerable seed who even manages to create gardens and cities of his own. The Spanish empire's outpost has been refounded, established as a new Canaan bearing the mark of its self-made creator.

If Otis's biblical comparisons are taken at face value, and within the last year of his life he broke with the idea of being an exemplar to lesser men, he had little to fear. Certainly he need not have worried about Chandler stealing his fame in a successful act of emulation. Chandler exemplified the self-made man as we have come to know him: a purely economic being, not concerned with community, with active political life, or even with inhabiting a public world. After Otis's death in 1914, Chandler wrote, "Men may die, but influences do not";[74] the influence he sought, however, was not the public model that his father-in-law had possessed. As Gottlieb and Wolt note: "Chandler was extremely adept at behind the scenes activities. Chandler was not a 'true believer' like Otis and could easily discard ideological positions if other objectives warranted it. Success in business matters provided the framework for Chandler's plans and his means were determined by those goals."[75]

The degree to which Otis's original plan, his vision of using emulation to create a metropolis of self-made men, had failed is clearest in the story of Harry Chandler: even among the elite of Los Angeles, even among those of enormous wealth and political connections, there was no one who would attempt to follow in the footsteps of Harrison Gray Otis. If, on the other hand, the language Otis used on the completion of the aqueduct was no more than excessive boasting, if he still conceived of himself at root as an exemplar of the self-made-man tradition, the end result was the same. The tradition died with him.

By the middle of the nineteenth century, the self-made man had become a popular replacement for the Roman statesman as the leading model for emulatory politics. Bridging the political and economic worlds, the self-made man was supposed to be natural and genuine, to tread new ground and be a genuine innovator, donning the role of a "natural and spontaneous" actor. The businessmen who succeeded in emulating this model were expected to present their lives as models for later generations of Americans. Harrison Gray Otis fulfilled this tradition to the letter; in the early history of Los Angeles, we have an ideal case study of the self-made man as an emulatory exercise. Otis's wars established the first successful Anglo movement for municipal reform in the Southland, an attempt to reform the character of the city imposed, as in the Philippines, through a military model. Some elite figures proved capable of emulating the self-made man; other citizens who did not attempt to emulate this model, who were content to settle for some degree of upward mobility within the middle class, were branded by Otis and his elites as potentially subversive of the exemplary city. The majority of Los Angeles citizens were thus locked out of Otis's political and economic elite public realm, unwilling or unable to follow in the publisher's footsteps and faced with coercion and models of quiescent submission to the city's leading citizens. To copy one who copies no one is an inherent impossibility, Hanna Pitkin reminds us.[76] The rhetoric of radical innovation, when chained to an impossible set of mimetic demands, undermines autonomy and prepares the ground for the sort of colonial mimesis described by Bhabha. Otis succeeded, in short, in refounding Los Angeles as an open-shop city in which public participation was narrowly defined as either the impossible emulation of his archetype or the submission of a depoliticized subject population.

Even those who succeeded in joining Otis's company, meanwhile, such as Harry Chandler, never saw the public realm of politics as inviting or interesting. Chandler and other "self-made men" of Southern California in the twentieth century concerned themselves with economic battles and remained in the background as much as possible. Such individuals did not present their lives as blueprints of virtue. Thus the first great experiment in political imitation in Los Angeles failed as an exercise in civic education, surviving only in the attenuated form of colonial mimicry and models of quiescence that a contemptuous Otis had once offered to the unambitious and "weak-kneed." The failure of Otis's model was not the end of experiments in political imitation, however. During World War II, the major Hollywood studios, working with the Roosevelt administration, promised to deliver the pedagogical combination of mass media and political exempla to mobilize the United States for a global war. It is to this battle that I now turn.

chapter 2

HOLLYWOOD IN THE 1940S
Emulation during Wartime

Even more striking is how vital a horizon of fantasy national culture remains, even to some radicals, in its promise of corporeal safety and the privacy of deep shadow.

—LAUREN BERLANT

The more performance scripts identity, the more it serves power.

—MICHAEL ROGIN

The symbol of the self-made man and its use as a legitimating ideology for the political and social structure of Southern California was embraced by the next generation of Los Angeles' media elite. The Hollywood studio system incorporated the vision of self-made virtue and the conservative promise of cultural mimicry in its most popular genres and went on to reach a national audience far beyond the scope of the *Los Angeles Times* or the All-Year Club. Yet Hollywood was also the site of the next great challenge to Otis's vision of civic virtue. The Great Depression destabilized the civic order imposed at the city's refounding, and the world war that followed transformed the politics and the content of Hollywood film. In the 1940s, Angelenos constructed new models of public life and carved out new meanings of civic virtue. New organizations, ad hoc coalitions, and alternate appeals to the authority of the American founding arose from the ruins of the war for Otistown. By the end of the 1940s, the struggle for a more agonal politics was once more undermined, as the core of Los Angeles' progressive community was suppressed beneath a tightly scripted vision of civic virtue. The heads of the studios, the "film moguls," promised to mirror the virtues of the Republic; film would enable citizens to mimic virtue, even if they had to be coerced into their roles. At midcentury, as at the city's refounding, the catalyst for this mimetic social order would be war. The Roosevelt administration mobilized the studios for service in World War II, and at the onset of the Cold War, the House of Representatives' Committee on Un-American Activities moved in to impose a model of colonial mimicry on the film community and the politicized Southland.

The Hollywood film industry in the 1930s and 1940s was divided into a number of studios, most of which produced films of differing genres and popular story lines.[1] Of all the major studios, MGM and Warner Brothers made films of the most unified and exhortatory styles, and the men in charge of these studios took the models they crafted to heart. Metro-Goldwyn-Mayer provided the most explicit ideal picture of citizenship, a bucolic picture of small-town virtue, but even that ideal formed the basis of only one genre among many. This was the ideal for which MGM is known, however, and it was the definition of citizen virtue that the studio adapted during the national mobilization of World War II. MGM would gratify its audience, studio president Louis B. Mayer promised, by demonstrating how virtuous audience members already were, and by reminding them to live up to that virtue. The studio would elevate through identity, not political action. This was a strategy Mayer devised at the onset of his career.

Louis B. Mayer was born in the Russian Ukraine in 1885, and his family emigrated to Canada two years later. Mayer's father, Jacob Meyer, made a scant living as a junk dealer, but he was a religious scholar and a respected figure in the Jewish community of St. Johns, New Brunswick. In later years, the successful studio chief described his childhood with the clichés of the self-made man, painting his father as a tyrannical failure whose inability to provide for the family forced his son to leave school at the age of twelve to travel throughout Canada buying scrap metal. Louis is, however, listed in the attendance rolls for the St. Johns High School through the age of seventeen.[2] Mayer's deviation from the requisite model of poverty and strenuous effort is unimportant. The rags-to-riches story of self-making was merely a prerequisite of the public role which he most wanted to play.

The nascent film industry provided Mayer with the means to establish legitimacy and wealth in his new country. After a brief period in Boston (where he married Margaret Shenberg, daughter of a middle-class rabbi), he settled in Haverhill, Massachusetts, and purchased an old burlesque theater on the waterfront of the expanding suburb. Mayer had lofty ambitions for himself and for the new medium; he was determined to show only "quality" films in an opulent venue, providing edifying family entertainment. Within two years, Mayer owned three theaters in Haverhill, where he put on theatrical productions and showed the films of Jesse Lasky's Famous Players in Famous Plays Studios. According to Irene Mayer Selznick, "He deplored the way show business was being run; he thought everyone in it had an obligation to make it respectable and keep it so."[3] Mayer was determined to use the virtues of an American small town—close-knit community, the family, and reverence for tradition—to improve the morals of the movies and then to close the circle, using the new ethical movie-viewing experience to mirror and increase the virtues of the small town. Mayer's studio, in fact, invented or significantly reinterpreted many of the traditions he professed to reflect, but he defined that innovation as an act of preservation. Citizens of the United States, Mayer argued, already possessed exemplary qualities but were in danger of forgetting them; the film industry would remind them of their moral birthright. The formula Mayer perfected in Haverhill would be the blueprint for the project he pursued in Hollywood.

By 1914, Mayer had tired of limiting himself to the exhibition of other people's films. He earned half a million dollars as the only licensed exhibitor of D. W. Griffith's *The Birth of a Nation* (1915) in New England, and he used the money to start a series of production and exhibition companies, including Louis B. Mayer Productions and Metro Pictures. In the span of four years he had signed Anita Stewart, one of the most popular movie stars in the country, and moved to Hollywood to devote himself to producing films. Once in Southern California, Mayer stumbled on a golden opportunity: Marcus Loew, who had made millions with a movie theater chain on the East Coast, decided to buy Goldwyn Studios, a small film company in Hollywood. Goldwyn's attorney, J. Robert Rubin, was also the attorney for Metro and a friend of Mayer; Rubin introduced Loew and Mayer, and Loew decided to purchase Metro and make Louis B. Mayer the president in charge of production for the Metro-Goldwyn-Mayer

Studio. Almost overnight, Mayer became one of the most influential figures in the film industry.[4]

Immediately upon the studio's founding, Mayer designed the MGM studio identification shot, the roaring lion under the legend "Ars Gratia Artis" (Art for art's sake). This was not an accurate statement of Mayer's aesthetic philosophy, however: MGM was charged with the task of creating art for *virtue's* sake. Mayer was intent on engaging American audiences in the imitation of exemplary American virtue. The studio motto was not meaningless, however. Using a motion picture studio to inculcate virtue would be next to impossible when many small-town citizens accused the industry of an inherent vulgarity and corruption. Mayer's dream required, therefore, a studio of unparalleled ethical and artistic respectability. He set about wooing the best talent he could find, using Loew's considerable fortune as an enticement.[5] While trying to hire director Lois Weber, Mayer promised her that "my unchanging policy will be great star, great director, great play, great cast. You are authorized to get these without stint or limit. Spare nothing, neither expense, time, nor effort. Results only are what I am after. Simply send me the bills and I will OK."[6] By and large, Mayer kept this promise, consistently producing movies that combined aesthetic quality with homespun tales of virtue in the American heartland. Mayer intended to spread his Haverhill project of imitation on a national level, using his studio to create an exemplar of the small-town virtues he wanted to proffer to viewers throughout the United States. "It has been my argument and practice," Mayer said at MGM's opening ceremony, "that each picture should teach a lesson, should have a reason for existence."[7] Mayer was going to teach a lesson in his ideal of small-town American virtue, and he wanted his employees and his audience to follow the model provided by that lesson closely.[8]

Although Louis B. Mayer did not share Harrison Gray Otis's zeal to personify a public exemplar of citizenship, he did struggle to ensure that the personal lives of his family and his stars did not undermine the ideals of his films. Shaping exemplary films required a publicly virtuous theatrical company.[9] Family was the primary institution of exemplary virtue in Mayer's fictional small towns, and Mayer saw himself as the patriarch as well as the president of his studio. He gave advice to all his employees, insisting that his actors dress, behave, and vote the right way. He excoriated

John Gilbert and Clark Gable when they cheated on their wives, held brunches at his home every Sunday for the families of MGM employees, and lectured Maureen O'Sullivan for not writing enough letters to her father.[10] When silent film star John Gilbert insulted his own mother, Mayer punched him.[11] He was obsessed with family relations as the basis of good character, integrating family scenes into movies, work relationships, and social functions. He even integrated family into the studio's editing process, telling directors during the silent era that he would not release movies that he could not show to his wife and daughters (and he initially had his family watch all of the MGM films before they were released).[12]

Crafting an exemplar required a constant theatricality. Mayer was perpetually conscious of being in the public eye, of needing to perform constantly in order to maintain his vision for MGM and the country. Indeed, he assumed a number of the studio's roles, acting out characters to show actors how it should be done. According to Mayer's daughter Edith, people in Hollywood "used to call him the D. W. Griffith of actors," and many opined that he was the best actor at MGM. He argued that he—and his family—needed such skills if they were to provide the model of citizenship that enabled the studio to provide national exempla.[13]

While crafting a model of virtue for his national audience, Mayer continued to grapple with Southern California's model of successful self-making. Working in a pattern perfected by Harrison Gray Otis and Harry Chandler, Mayer created a network of financial relationships across the Southland. Between 1924 (when he became president of MGM) and 1937, Mayer purchased shares in four other studios (United Artists, Selznick International Pictures, Radio-Keith Orpheum, and Fox Studios) and further connected himself with the elite of the film community by entering into extensive real estate syndicates. By the time of the stock market crash of 1929, Mayer had protected his fortune by joining Nicholas Schenck, president of MGM's parent company, Loew's, Incorporated, and MGM vice president Irving Thalberg in the purchase of real estate throughout Southern California.[14] He and Thalberg fought any attempt at unionization at the studio, threatening and firing organizers and participating in the founding of the famous company union, the Motion Picture Academy of the Arts and Sciences. He also devoted himself to the Republican Party and became a fund-raiser for, and friend of, Herbert Hoover.[15] After

Hoover's election, Mayer accepted the position of chair of the California Republican Committee at the president's urging, but declined the post of ambassador to Turkey, a traditional token Jewish position. Mayer told people that he had lost his birth certificate, and that he had adopted July 4 as his birthday; assimilation was his goal, not the marked difference of a token position. Mayer's ambitions, however, were doomed to failure. The producer was among the highest-paid people in the country and remained almost an exemplary citizen in the Otis fashion—but not quite. A Jewish immigrant with a mimetic devotion to American narratives of virtue, Mayer committed himself to preserving a vision of civic community to which he could never fully belong.

In 1936, Irving Thalberg, MGM vice president in charge of production and Mayer's partner in politics and real estate, died of heart failure. In the preceding decade he and Mayer had crafted a great reputation for MGM.[16] *Ben-Hur* (1925), *The Big Parade* (1925), *Grand Hotel* (1932), and *Mutiny on the Bounty* (1935) all typify Thalberg's projects: expensive films, lavishly produced and carefully crafted. From the lot in Culver City where Mayer worked to appear as the caring patriarch of all his employees to the stages where Loew's money had bought the best directors, writers, and stars, to the screening rooms where Thalberg viewed mountains of footage and demanded scores of retakes, MGM became famous as the exemplar of aesthetic respectability in the film community. After Thalberg's death, Mayer redoubled his efforts to provide a model for the education and imitation of the enormous MGM audience. Now that the legitimacy of MGM was apparently beyond dispute, Mayer turned from the aesthetically polished models of virtue that had characterized the better films of the Thalberg period (Sydney Carton of *A Tale of Two Cities,* for example). The MGM films that characterized the late 1930s were populated by "everyday" heroes who experienced melodrama at a distance. Mayer argued that his homespun heroes would show American audiences the way to ethical citizenship. The characters he proffered were insulated from challenges even within the film story lines they inhabited, however. Remote from public struggle, Mayer's exempla were at most passive conservators of a privatized world. The most striking example of this model and its weaknesses was also Mayer's favorite character: Andy Hardy.

"The Andy Hardy pictures," Mayer stated in an interview near the end of his life, "were the best pictures ever."[17] The B-picture series, starring

Mickey Rooney as a "typical American teenager," was extremely profitable. Rooney was voted "the most popular performer" in Hollywood for 1939, 1940, and 1941, and the studio produced seven of the Andy Hardy films in just two years (1938 and 1939). Mayer was not alone in claiming that the series reflected essential virtues of the American Republic; the series received a special Academy Award "for its achievement in representing the American Way of Life."[18]

During the early 1930s, Mayer was concerned that Irving Thalberg's devotion to literary adaptations and portraits of glamorous beauty was preempting his own vision for the studio. In the years immediately following Thalberg's death, therefore, the Andy Hardy series represented a concerted attempt on Mayer's part to provide his own ideal vision of the United States. He insisted on seeing the rushes of each scene and consistently interfered with series producer Carey Wilson. In addition to Mayer's involvement, the uniform message and vision of the series was further ensured by the use of the same director, George Seitz, on all fifteen films.[19] The Hardy films exemplify Mayer's project of imitation: the movies reflect back an imagined world of homespun virtue—community, strong families, and reverence for tradition—and invite audiences to follow that model. Audiences similar to the Hardys imitate Hollywood glamour and paradoxically are led back to the recognition of their inherent virtues and an easy imitation of American exempla. Thus Andy Hardy imitates models—his father, glamorous celebrities[20]—with which he will never be able to compete, and that serve only to lead him back to his own childish and submissive position; he is insulated from public struggle or emulatory competition. Mayer defines Andy as a central subject of the American experience yet constructs him through the assimilationist process of colonial mimesis.

The series takes place largely in the fictional hamlet of Carvel. The town has a clear set of authority figures, but none is more symbolic of patriarchal authority than Andy's father, Judge Hardy (Lewis Stone). Andy attempts to fix an adult identity for himself, chasing the signs of maturity (romance and cars, largely) using the opposed models of big-city glamour and his father's social position. The world represented by Hollywood, the realm of drama and celebrity, provides the clearest model for the youth of Carvel in *Andy Hardy Gets Spring Fever* (1939). Infatuated with a new drama teacher, Andy melds Shakespeare with South Seas adventure films, writing a play (*Adrift in Tahiti*) that the drama class performs. The attempt of small-town youth to imitate Hollywood productions was a staple of MGM genres by the late 1930s; it forms the story line of a significant number of "Our Gang" two-reelers and of the popular musical *Babes in Arms* (1939), costarring Rooney and Judy Garland. Just as Mayer, in his opinion, increased the virtue of small Haverhill by bringing movies to it, the world of Hollywood films entered the small towns of the Hardys and Our Gang, providing a model that would safely guide them through the world outside. Asked by his drama teacher how he created such a "clever" play, Andy replies, "I took *Romeo and Juliet* and changed it a little bit . . . uh . . . I moved it from Italy to a South Sea island, and I took Romeo and made him a rear admiral and naturally I had to change Juliet to a pretty little South Sea island native girl, and then I wrote a whole new plot! I think my ending is better than Shakespeare's. It's more spiritual." In his mind, Andy has imitated Shakespeare and improved on him; Hollywood and his own romantic disappointment have allowed him to emulate the Bard successfully, and to achieve fame and glory.

Adrift in Tahiti is awful, of course; even Andy's proud parents are amused by their son's clumsy attempt at tragedy. Andy's primary models in *Spring Fever* (Judge Hardy and the MGM jungle romance/adventure films)[21] shield him from the need to try to grapple with the issues that underlie his tragic play. Likewise, it is a condition of his imitative endeavors that he not struggle with the difficult adult world. It is a staple of the Hardy films that Andy brings his problems to his father for a "man-to-man" talk, and when Andy offers to have a "man-to-man talk" with a younger schoolmate at the end of the film, we know that he is trying to walk in his father's footsteps. Nonetheless, in each film Judge Hardy attempts to ensure that his son will *never* have to struggle with his example.

MGM films insist that the imitation of virtue is easy. The security of the American small town is like a buffer between citizens and the difficulties and dangers of the modern world; the models provided by the small town suggest that virtue is achieved through passivity. Judge Hardy is one of Carvel's leading citizens, providing the townspeople with the sort of benign guidance that he provides for his son. The townspeople's problems are more serious than Andy's, however. In *Spring Fever*, Carvel's main crisis is a successful confidence game that takes in the judge and most of the town's elite. The judge must figure out a way to save his family's economic position and good name while also protecting the rest of the investors. He still takes time out to listen to Andy's problems, however, and to intervene with the object of his son's affections, drama teacher Rose Meredith: "I guess every parent dreads the day when his child will get his first real hurt. I'm putting myself at your mercy; you'll know the right thing to do." In other words, the Hardy patriarch's main object in this and the other films is to shield his son and his fellow citizens from the struggles and disillusionment that he deals with in every film, yet when he is faced with the problem of his "child's first real hurt," he responds by surrendering. The crisis that affects the judge and the rest of the town's adults, meanwhile, is hidden from the teenagers. Thus, although Mayer proffers the Hardy films as a view on "the American Way of Life" that can "teach a lesson,"[22] he presents an America where the clichés of film provide models for imitative youth that are buffered from the struggle inherent in the imitation of republican virtues. Mayer's imitative schema is a call to passivity: MGM's models of small-town virtue are a young man who experiences life by imitating an aesthetic reflection of himself and a benign parent who conceals his own generally passive struggles from the public world.

Even when Andy Hardy leaves Carvel for New York, in 1940's *Andy Hardy Meets Debutante,* he remains safely ensconced in MGM's ideal small-town America. This series entry presents both Hardy men succumbing to despair in the big city, rescued only by the inherent conservatism of Mayer's concept of political art. The public models of MGM, the exempla of small-town virtue, are not demanding, Mayer demonstrates, because they only remind us of our own inherent nature. The differences between Carvel and New York City are superficial; the good citizen must only recognize that fact and embrace his inherited ethical standards.

Debutante features Judy Garland in one of her three appearances in the series as Betsy Booth. As Robert Ray points out, Betsy mediates between the familiar world of Carvel and the metropolis: "True, Betsy *is* shy, selfless, awkward, and, above all, younger than Andy; but as a rich New Yorker, the daughter of a famous theatrical actress, and a hot singer in her own right, she is also, as Andy admits after the dance, 'sensational.'"[23] Betsy is a last-minute savior in *Debutante,* the film in which Andy and the judge disparage the virtuous existence of the American small town.

Andy's mission in the city is to get a picture with "New York's leading debutante," Daphne Fowler, to avoid humiliation in Carvel, where he had bragged that the celebrity was "crazy about" him. Fowler does not know him, however, and he initially fails to meet her due to his inability to enter the world of Manhattan's wealthy elite. He becomes embittered, losing faith in the small-town American ethos of hard work and self-making. Even Judge Hardy's advice is incapable of raising Andy's spirits. When the judge takes Andy to see the New York University Hall of Fame, he hopes to shame his son into honoring his political inheritance ("I never thought I'd hear you, my own son, deny the very soil you walk on, soil that was earned for you by the blood and sweat of men who said that all men should be created equal"). His admonition is met by a bitter tirade from Andy: "That was fine a hundred years ago, when a guy had a chance, but now there's millions of people like us! Here in New York I'm just a hick with delusions of grandeur and you're just a country judge that no one's ever heard of."

The judge's New York adventure parallels Andy's. Americans' inability to recognize their own virtuous superiority threatens to become a self-fulfilling prophesy: a former trustee for the Carvel orphanage, Harlan Wyatt, lost faith in America's superiority during the Great Depression and traded the orphanage's U.S. Treasury bonds for European bonds. The advent of war in Europe ruined the orphanage. Despairing after his meeting with Andy and looking bitterly at the Statue of Liberty, the judge tells his wife, "This city's got me licked . . . and all because Harlan Wyatt lost faith in his own country. I guess this town's too big for me."

The problems are resolved by the discovery of the underlying similarity between Carvel and New York City. Betsy Booth turns out to be close friends with Daphne Fowler, who, in turn, is a "regular girl" who likes to collect butterflies and has to wear special long underwear because of allergies; she is only too happy to have her picture taken fawning over Andy. The resolution to the orphanage problem occurs to the judge after he talks the problem over with Mrs. Hardy and consults his old law books; the issue is easy to prove in court, where the New York judge and attorneys are happy to help save the children's money. The solutions to the Hardys' big-city problems were with them all the time, carried out of Carvel and preserved by the small-town virtues of good people in the big city.

Judge Hardy and the fictional world of the movies serve to protect Andy from the world outside, but that world is actually quite similar to Carvel. The point of the Hardy series, and of many of MGM's films, is to remind people of what qualities in their own characters they should most esteem; the studio provides this service by showing them those virtues in the actors on the screen. For Washington, Lincoln, and Otis, emulation is a political struggle and a civic responsibility to be undertaken only by the right sort of citizen, whereas the mimicry of simplistic models can be forced on subject audiences. Mayer promises, in contrast, that virtuous American citizens will not have to struggle with their models. Audience members become virtuous by imitating characters that are like themselves, only more removed from the struggles of the day. The point of imitation in the MGM canon is not to struggle with one's models, but to let one's models help one to remember, to fall back into the virtuous state of small-town America.

One critic sees the comic conclusion of *Life Begins for Andy Hardy* (1941) to be a particularly telling moment for the ideology of the series. At the film's beginning, Andy has graduated from high school, sold his beloved jalopy, and moved to the big city; by the end of the film he has returned to Carvel and is working happily on his car once more. "Reunited with Betsy and his parents, at the wheel of his 'repaired' jalopy, Andy shifts triumphantly into third gear and finds the car moving rapidly, violently *backwards*."[24] But Mayer's message in the Hardy series is not that America should turn the clock back. The models that Mayer, his family, and his studio purported to embrace and to provide were not historically remote; despite the prestige historical dramas of the Thalberg era, MGM did not call on its audiences to struggle with the example of the American founders. Mayer argued that the virtues of small-town America still exist, and that the "reason for [his films'] existence" is to serve as models of those virtues, to remind audiences that they really know how they should behave. Mayer intended to use film to replicate the essential virtues that he claimed to maintain in his family and his studio. Otis had urged passivity on the majority of Angelenos while arguing that the elite group to which he belonged should struggle to emulate self-made leaders. Mayer provides a passive model, a vision of American virtue to which *he* is attempting to assimilate.

This conservative standard of imitative action is also the moral of another popular MGM film with Judy Garland from 1939: *The Wizard of Oz*. Based on the 1900 children's novel *The Wonderful Wizard of Oz*, by L. Frank Baum, the musical exemplified Mayer's standard of mimetic virtue. The Scarecrow, the Tin Woodsman, and the Cowardly Lion are all possessed of the qualities they think they lack; in Peter Glassman's words, they possess "unrealized virtues."[25] Just as the clever Scarecrow thinks he needs brains, or as the compassionate Woodsman thinks he needs a heart, Dorothy Gale always has but does not recognize the qualities that she most desires. At the film's beginning, Dorothy thinks that she needs to explore the world in order to be happy; despite the Technicolor adventure of Oz, she then spends most of the film trying to return to the monochromatic Kansas prairie. Reciting the film's "lesson" to Glinda the Good Witch, Dorothy ensures that the audience will learn it too: "If I ever go looking for my heart's desire again, I won't look any further than my own backyard, because if it isn't there, I never really lost it to begin with." Indeed, when Dorothy wakes up at the end of the film, the audience realizes that she never left Kansas at all. Just as Garland as Betsy Booth mediates the two worlds of Andy Hardy by consciously bringing the values of Carvel to the heart of upper-class Manhattan, Garland's Dorothy carries her Kansas devotion to family and good manners with her wherever she goes.

The Wizard of Oz—and, indeed, all of the MGM productions of which Mayer was most proud—is designed to perform the same function as Dorothy's trip to Oz. Dorothy serves as a model by which Mayer can "instill values in the country" through film.[26] As Garland does in her MGM performances, so the audience must do, acting with the virtues of small-town America wherever they are if they are to serve as ideal citizens. Thomas Jefferson argued that art could serve to instruct citizens in public virtue.[27] Mayer used his popular art to instruct citizens in a static vision of identity, urging them merely to recognize and submit to, not emulate or struggle with, civic virtue. All models at MGM, furthermore, were derived from private life. The only virtuous public arena in Mayer's ideal America was Judge Hardy's courtroom.

Warner Brothers Studios, whose motto was "Combining Good Picture Making with Good Citizenship," produced a coherent vision of U.S. culture that was politically and aesthetically opposed to the MGM ideal. Where Mayer founded his studio on a promise of high aesthetic standards, Warner Brothers made a virtue out of low budgets. While Mayer and Thalberg perfected the silent movie, pushing "the American film industry in the last years of the silent era" to "reach its peak of artistic and commercial achievement,"[28] Warner Brothers rang the death knell for silent film with the groundbreaking "talkie," *The Jazz Singer* (1927). Mayer asserted that he reflected the realities of American life by celebrating small-town virtue; Jack Warner boasted that his studio mirrored the events he found in the crime pages of big-city newspapers. Warner Brothers released films designed to encourage certain forms of "good citizenship," but its models were creatures of an urban world that was different, faster, and far more dangerous than the homespun villages praised by Mayer.

Harry and Jack Warner may have defined themselves against the vision of virtue proffered by Mayer, but not against the concept of ideal virtuous citizenship per se. Harry, the studio's president, was characterized by *Fortune* magazine as having "two major interests: business and morals." He wanted to use his position to increase religious tolerance and to spread a more inclusive definition of virtuous citizenship.[29] Indeed, Warner's philosophy of filmmaking was comparable to Mayer's in its emphasis on creating virtue in audiences. He "believe[d] that all Warner pictures carry some moral lesson. 'The motion picture,' he says simply, 'presents right

In *The Wizard of Oz* (1939), Dorothy Gale (Judy Garland) learns her lesson: "If I ever go looking for my heart's desire again, I won't look any further than my own backyard, because if it isn't there, I never really lost it to begin with."

and wrong, as the Bible does. By showing both right and wrong we teach the right.'"[30] Harry argued that the gangster and "social problem" films that were Warner Brothers' specialties provided a multitude of models, reflecting the political life of the nation, presenting human villains that audiences could empathize with but learn to shun, heroes for audiences to learn from and follow, and the larger social problems with which all citizens had to struggle.

The Warner brothers were also comparable to Mayer in the passive and private nature of their vision of civic life. "In the movie colony, as in the movies themselves," wrote Leo Rosten, "romantic individualism, the most compelling idea in American history, has reached the apogee of its glory."[31] The rugged individual as a liberal symbol of the underdog was the classic Warners persona. Such heroes are a far cry from the sheltered protagonists at Metro. Nonetheless, this view of citizenship and heroism does not stray far from the same central tenets of the definition of citizenship proffered by Otis and Mayer. At Warner Brothers, the individual was not the self-made patriarch of the *Los Angeles Times,* but despite the Warners films' partisan differences from MGM, they shared a common implicit conservative impulse of passive withdrawal and depoliticization.[32]

The Warners' answer to the blithe nostalgia of films such as *The Wizard of Oz* and Selznick's *Gone with the Wind* was Michael Curtiz's *Angels with Dirty Faces,* released in November 1938. James Cagney plays Rocky Sullivan, another version of the likable gangster he had been portraying in Warners films since *The Public Enemy* in 1931. Sullivan first appears as a teenager, walking the streets of New York City with his best friend, Jerry Connolly. The two attempt a minor theft; Sullivan is caught and sent to reform school. Rocky is loyal and friendly, obviously a boy victimized by a bad education and the surfeit of criminal role models he will meet in Juvenile Hall. Connolly, who escapes the police, embraces the Catholic Church and grows up to be a priest. The models that surround them decide the fates of both men.

When the adult Rocky returns to New York, Jerry—now Father Connolly (Pat O'Brien)—is attempting to shepherd a group of adolescents (the Dead End Kids from the play and film of the same name) he is trying to rescue from a life of crime. The two men resume their friendship. Rocky's virtues—his loyalty to old friends and desire to help teach the Kids— underscore the danger of the criminal models that were strong enough to lead him astray. Indeed, Rocky's successful rise in the criminal world (the audience learns about his exploits through newspaper headlines) replicates the efforts of the self-made man. Connolly recognizes this; he complains to Rocky that there are "criminals on all sides for my boys to look up to and revere and respect and admire and imitate." Rocky tries to help, using his influence with the boys to convince them to join the Church Athletic League, but his position as mentor is inherently problematic. In order to save the Dead End Kids from his own example, Rocky must follow the Warner Brothers credo: he must "show the wrong . . . to teach the right."

At the film's conclusion, Rocky is on death row. He is not frightened; he is stoically, indeed arrogantly, prepared to die. The Dead End Kids know this and exult in the fact that their hero will "show dem bums how to die." For this reason, Connolly asks Rocky for a last favor: that he die a cowardly death. "You've been a hero to these kids and hundreds of others. . . . Now you're going to be a glorified hero in death and I want to prevent that, Rocky. They've got to despise your memory, they've got to be ashamed of you." Rocky at first refuses; his carefully crafted persona is "the only thing I got left, the only thing they could never take away from me," but in the end he abides by the priest's request. In a chilling scene, he begs, pleads, and claws at a radiator while the news media report on the scene. The ruse works; the Dead End Kids abandon their worship of the gangster and return with Connolly to the church.

The film does not conclude with a clear victory for Connolly, however. One man has accepted his fate while a negative model has been discredited. We cannot be sure that the priest will convince even a majority of the Kids to adopt the models of civic virtue that Harry Warner wanted to teach. We do not see the teens attempt to imitate Connolly or the film's bumbling policemen. The film's audience, meanwhile, is privy to Rocky's sacrifice; he remains the most attractive model in the story. *Angels with Dirty Faces* is far less reactionary and protective of its audience than the typical MGM film, but it shares with Mayer's work an implicit political pessimism. Its most attractive character remains the doomed lone protagonist, not the adherent of activist liberalism that the Warner brothers favored in their partisan politics. The audience for *Angels* was unlikely to be persuaded to emulate Father Connolly or to imitate any models of active republican citizenship.

The solitary rugged hero may not be a political or religious actor, but he is not necessarily a criminal. In 1941, for example, Warner Brothers drew on a classic of "hard-boiled" detective fiction to produce a film that epitomized the studio's prewar style: John Huston's production of *The Maltese Falcon.* Unlike *Angels, Falcon* does not represent a story of the power of imitation. I include it in this discussion rather because it clearly demonstrates the type of character that Warner Brothers films idealized and that the studio would adapt convincingly in its wartime emulatory films.[33] Father Jerry Connolly was too noble, too sacred, for the Warners audience—or the Warners themselves—to choose over Rocky Sullivan, but Dashiell Hammett's hero was a figure worth imitating. Sam Spade (Humphrey Bogart) is on the side of law and order, but for much of the film there is little aside from the character's professionalism to separate him from the criminal world in which he moves. His reaction to the murder of his partner, Miles Archer, is cold and utilitarian.[34] He assumes that the world around him is duplicitous and dangerous and that he must deal with it. Further, despite a flirtatious friendship with his secretary and working relationships with policemen, cab drivers, and hotel security men across San Francisco, he is a solitary figure, working alone and not letting anyone (including the film's audience) know what he is thinking. He is tough, highly professional, and alone.

This professionalism is made clear at the film's conclusion. At several points in the movie, Spade's allegiances and motives are unclear, but after he calls the police to arrange the arrests of the gang responsible for most of the crimes in the movie, his role as hero is made explicit. The film's penultimate scene is played between Spade and his love interest, Brigid O'Shaughnessy (Mary Astor). O'Shaughnessy, Spade reveals, murdered Miles Archer. Despite the facts that he did not like Archer and was sleeping with Archer's wife, Spade is now determined to surrender his lover to the police for reasons that combine the individualistic ethos and the dedication to an ethical code that mark Warner Brothers protagonists:

> When a man's partner is killed he's supposed to do something about it. It doesn't make any difference what you thought of him. He was your partner and you're supposed to do something about it. Then it happens we were in the detective business. Well, when one of your organization gets killed it's bad business to let the killer get away with it. It's bad all around, bad for that one organization, bad for every detective everywhere. . . . Maybe you

love me and maybe I love you. . . . I'll have some rotten nights after I send
you over, but that'll pass.

Bogart looks sick as he delivers these lines; Spade is obviously not cavalier
about sending O'Shaughnessy to the gallows. He seems no more triumph-
ant than Father Connolly does when he achieves his goals. Nonetheless, he is bound by a professional code, and being alone is intrinsic to his
character, so the audience is sure that he will, in fact, get over the "rotten
nights."

This is a different picture of the film hero than we have seen before, but
there are also striking similarities with the film world of MGM. Dorothy
Gale and Judge Hardy are exultant in their ability to remain static, to have
no change in their situations or the situations of their family and friends,
and this can hardly be said of Father Connolly and Sam Spade. Nonetheless, if the Warners heroes are merely acquiescing to a situation that the
MGM heroes are celebrating, they are still not rebelling against it. The
world around them remains the same; the actions they take are merely
reactions to events. The priest does not question that the young will
merely mimic the most glamorous model they have; he only hopes to
discredit that model. The detective does not even attempt to reform or
transform a world whose mendaciousness and violence he takes for granted;
he lives by a code to make sure that he does not harm himself or other
detectives. Despite the difference in affect between MGM's product and
Warner Brothers', one could argue that this is a general characteristic of
prewar Hollywood film. Claiming to reflect important characteristics of
American culture, the studio moguls proffered a static ideal of public life.
Indeed, as was also the case with MGM, Warner Brothers' ideal public
world was inhabited only by the models of private life. It is private detective Spade, not the corrupt politicians or policemen of the Warner Brothers films, who serves as an exemplar. This is the code of ethics that Warner
Brothers would have to adapt for wartime; maintaining its characters'
individualism, the studio would have to expand the code that, in this
instance, is limited to the restricted world of detectives to the larger realm
of the citizen body.

Within weeks of December 7, 1941, the president of the United States
called on the Hollywood moguls to break the privatized pattern of political imitation that characterized pre-war film. During the war, MGM and

Warner Brothers were forced to transform their most characteristic prewar genres, but without, I will argue, altering the central lesson of their cinematic pedagogy; even at its most exhortative, wartime Hollywood film remained embedded in a democratic rhetoric of mimetic stasis.

Even before the United States entered World War II, the conflict in Europe was threatening the status quo that the major studios' prewar output had assumed. Franklin Delano Roosevelt's Fireside Chat on September 3, 1939, addressed the question of the war in Europe: "This nation will remain a neutral nation, but I cannot ask that every American remain neutral in thought as well. Even a neutral has a right to take account of facts. Even a neutral cannot be asked to close his mind or close his conscience."[35] Jack and Harry Warner interpreted this message as an invitation for Hollywood to act independently as the conscience for the nation. The brothers dispatched a telegram to Roosevelt that read, in part, "Personally we would like to do all in our power within the motion picture industry and by use of the talking screen to show the American people the worthiness of the cause for which the free peoples of Europe are making such tremendous sacrifices."[36]

The Warner brothers' action preceded any similar actions on the part of other studio moguls by as much as two years, but the commitment to educate Americans about fascism ran throughout much of the Hollywood creative community. With Roosevelt's election and the beginning of the civil war in Spain, political activism in Hollywood had increased dramatically. An independent political arena was difficult to initiate in Southern California. Otis and the Merchants and Manufacturers' Association had fought to disable any political movement that opposed the publisher's refounding vision. Organized labor was foremost among Otis's enemies, and the moguls had fought with other Los Angeles elites against the attempt to increase unionization at the onset of the Depression. Indeed, as Larry Ceplair and Steven Englund describe in their outstanding history of political struggle in Hollywood, it was "President Roosevelt's Bank Holiday in March 1933—which launched the New Deal—[that] persuaded studio management to resurrect the old deal of paternalistic labor/management relations which the Motion Picture Academy had been created to camouflage."[37] At MGM, Mayer—"the best actor on the lot"— wept while telling employees that he would be imposing a 50 percent salary cut in order to ensure the survival of the studio. The revelation the following year that the studio was financially quite successful, and that Mayer and Thalberg continued to make record salaries, initiated efforts by some studio employees (particularly screenwriters) to create unions. The studio moguls branded the early steps toward union organization as disloyal, subversive, and communistic. Even New Dealers Harry and Jack Warner adhered to the antiunion line, bringing in strikebreakers and engaging in red-baiting in the *Los Angeles Times* and elsewhere. Only the intervention of the federal government and the newly created National Labor Relations Board were capable of forcing Mayer and the Warner brothers to recognize the unions, whose legitimacy they remained unwilling to accept.

The greatest factor in mobilizing Hollywood labor, however, was the behavior of the studios during the 1934 California gubernatorial election. In some ways, the Depression had re-created some of the circumstances of the final years of the Otistown wars: economic crisis and an apparent lack of a legitimate conservative strategy to deal with it led to the very real possibility of a socialist elected official. According to Ceplair and Englund, "By June 1934, 700,000 workers were unemployed in California, half of them in Los Angeles county, where one fifth of all residents barely subsisted on welfare (at the rate of $16.20 per month)."[38] Upton Sinclair, former Socialist Party candidate for a number of state offices, switched party registration and became the Democratic Party's candidate for governor of California. Sinclair's platform was relatively mild—his proposed reforms were not unlike those being suggested by Roosevelt's brain trust—but large companies throughout the state reacted with alarm. The *Los Angeles Times,* the *Examiner,* and studio newsreel units used stock footage of tramps jumping freight cars bound for California and Sinclair's "Bolshevik" paradise, presenting the mini-melodramas as reportage. The moguls threatened to move their studios to Florida and began automatically deducting "campaign contributions" to Republican gubernatorial candidate Frank Merriam from employees' paychecks. Sinclair lost the election, but the anger of Hollywood employees mobilized union organization to an unprecedented degree, and the activism of California progressives, liberals, and radicals accelerated. Groups of people who had been effectively depoliticized since the Otistown wars reengaged in politics, moving from the fight over Upton Sinclair to the fight to raise money and material support for the war against fascism in Europe and at home.[39]

Among writers, actors, and some directors, the social world of the film community was transformed into a buzz of committees and fund-raising societies. Screenwriter Mary McCall jocularly complained:

> We're up to our necks in politics and morality now. Nobody goes to anybody's house any more to sit and talk and have fun. There's a master of ceremonies and a collection basket, because there are no gatherings except for a Good Cause. We have almost no time to be actors or writers these days. We're committee members and collectors and organizers and audiences for orators.[40]

The committees worked to good effect: speeches by writers Ernest Hemingway and John Dos Passos and screenings of documentaries such as *The Spanish Earth* (1937) raised thousands of dollars. "Hollywood," in the words of Ian Hamilton, "became the place where any anti-fascist movement went for dollars."[41] In 1936, a number of film community luminaries, including Melvyn Douglas, Donald Ogden Stewart, Dorothy Parker, and Philip Dunne, formed the Hollywood Anti-Nazi League. By 1939, the league was joined by a variety of other liberal and left-wing political organizations, supporting Roosevelt and working against international and domestic fascism as the Popular Front.[42]

Studio heads with outlets and investments in Europe were in no hurry to antagonize Hitler's government, but an increasing number of producers began supporting intervention in the war, including the Warners, independent producers Daryl Zanuck and Samuel Goldwyn, and Paramount executive Walter Wanger.[43] By mid-1940, film executives had formed the Motion Picture Committee Cooperating for National Defense "to coordinate the industry with outside groups in the national emergency" and to distribute informational films on the situation in Europe provided by the Roosevelt administration.[44] Loew's president Nicholas Schenck offered Roosevelt the use of the MGM studio.

The open cooperation between the major studios and the Roosevelt administration elicited strenuous protests from conservatives and isolationists in the U.S. Congress. Democratic Senators Burton Wheeler (Montana) and Gerald Nye (North Dakota) of the Committee on Interstate Commerce argued that Hollywood was engaged in a propaganda campaign to induce Americans to enter the war in Europe. Nye's vision of the workings of media was antithetical to that of the Warner brothers and

Mayer. Harrison Gray Otis no doubt would have welcomed an instantly malleable population in his ideal city, but he found that crossing racial and class divides with his mimetic models of difference engendered resistance. Nye, Wheeler, and other isolationists in Congress feared that such resistance would work in only one direction, and that American audiences would prove easier to colonize, adapting themselves unconsciously to the roles they saw on the screen. Nye argued that Hollywood was a participant in a politics of conspiracy and biological compulsion, that the Jewish owners of the major studios were "naturally susceptible to racial emotions," and that the "cunning" hidden messages of Hollywood film would brainwash audiences who thought they were only receiving entertainment.[45]

The studios countered with ringing defenses of their films and their audiences. Harry Warner summed up the studio argument in his testimony before Wheeler's War Propaganda Subcommittee. Wheeler had charged that "Warner Brothers is producing pictures concerning world affairs and national defense [that are] inaccurate and twisted for ulterior purpose." Harry Warner countered that the anti-Nazi films "show the world as it is." "If that is propaganda," Warner declared, "we plead guilty." Interestingly, Warner denied that his studio was exhorting citizens. Warner Brothers was merely reflecting reality, as it had always done. If audiences reacted to that reality differently now, their reaction was due to their own patriotism and bravery, not to biological or conspiratorial control. The other studios echoed Warner's argument. Furthermore, film industry counsel Wendell Wilkie argued, the so-called propaganda films were "exceedingly good" pictures that audiences wanted to see. The studio chiefs employed a favorite argument at the hearing: Hollywood was using popular films to educate citizens in public virtue. Lastly, Warner added, it was erroneous to claim that a conspiracy existed between the studio heads and President Roosevelt: the major studios had made a number of films "portraying the lives of American heroes. To do this, we needed no urging from the government and we would be ashamed if the government would have to make such requests of us."[46]

Warner's defense of the studios illustrates Hollywood's ambiguous approach to its attempts at defining wartime virtue. The studio moguls were willing to provide models of heroic citizens, but they insisted that they were only presenting a mimetic picture of the nation, and that they were doing so dutifully. The deference of the studios to patriotic necessity, their audience, and the "world as it is" illustrates the problem of imitation as a political tool: without an emulatory commitment to agonal public struggle, the imitator must either fail to measure up to exempla or adopt the conservator's attitude seen in Lincoln and Cicero. The mimetic subject is almost, but not quite, a real civic actor, as Bhabha reminds us; when mimesis becomes a goal for the subject population, the gap between exemplar and imitator is consciously preserved and even widened. As the political differences between MGM and Warner Brothers were largely superficial, so were the differences between prewar and wartime film. In the last analysis, Hollywood's most cohesive and influential studios flirted with propaganda and even emulatory models in their war films while remaining faithful to an implicitly passive vision of republican virtue. Indeed, from Machiavelli's exhortation to re-create Rome to Cicero's pieties to Otis's attempt to found an ideal city, this has been a central tension of emulatory pedagogy: at the heart of the democratic educational project, we find a consistent exhortation to static investment in a pre-existing hierarchy. "This," and nothing else, "*is* the city."

The war in Europe increased the use of an exhortatory rhetoric of public struggle in the studios' products, however. In part, this was a reflection of the increased influence of the Popular Front and the fact that segments of Los Angeles society that had been dedicated to political action for years were suddenly able to act on that commitment with the blessing of the Southland's social and economic elites. This escalation of oratory was also assisted—even organized—by the Roosevelt administration's propaganda arm, the Office of War Information. In their exhaustive book on Hollywood politics during World War II, Koppes and Black define propaganda as

the expression of opinion or actions carried out deliberately by individuals or groups with a view to influencing the opinions or actions of other individuals or groups for predetermined ends and through psychological manipulation . . . [and presented with] a steady pervasive repetition [that] creates a field from which the individual finds it hard to stand back and form an independent judgment.[47]

Prewar Hollywood film had too many genres and moral lessons to present the solitary "field" that Koppes and Black describe. The president and the OWI would attempt to unify these genres and moral lessons around singular wartime exempla, much as Otis had imposed order on an earlier generation of entrepreneurs.

Roosevelt created the OWI in June 1942 "to undertake campaigns to enhance public understanding of the war at home and abroad; to coordinate government information activities; and to handle liaison with the press, radio, and motion pictures."[48] Liaisons Lowell Mellett and Nelson Poynter set up OWI offices at Hollywood and Vine and began the process of attempting to orchestrate Hollywood's treatment of the war effort. They did not have the power to force any of the studios to change scripts or finished products, but they did have power over the release of films internationally, which, even during wartime, accounted for a significant portion of studio income.[49]

OWI's first goal was to integrate the model of wartime patriotism into all mainstream films, and not just informational shorts and war movies. The major studios had created very specific and well-known visions of American life, and Mellett and Poynter endeavored to make the necessities of wartime citizenship an unavoidable part of those visions. Thus OWI chief Elmer Davis bluntly stated that "war propaganda" would have to be "casually and naturally introduced into the ordinary dialogue, business and scenes which constitute the bulk of film footage."[50] Comedies and romance films did not have to be *about* the war, but street scenes should have extras in uniform and war-related posters in shop windows. Films should include references to women getting jobs to help out at home, teenagers and children collecting rubber, and consumers cheerfully complying with food rationing, and no one should be shown wasting any important materials. OWI objected to film depictions of squealing tires, unnecessary train travel, and any apparent resentment toward the wealthy from the working-class characters. The nation's citizenry had to be mobilized for duty, and every aspect of film was to be affected. Thus Warner Brothers cartoon character Bugs Bunny would leap off a train at the end of a short because "we aren't supposed to do any unnecessary traveling," and MGM's Our Gang would stop performing in make-believe movies and start putting on make-believe USO shows and tin and rubber drives.

Late in the summer of 1942, OWI released a manual to help the movie studios present the proper set of goals for wartime citizens.[51] The studios took the manual seriously, distributing copies to all levels of production staff. To many observers, especially those who had been isolationist before the war, it seemed that Wheeler's and Nye's fears had been well-founded; although there was no secret conspiracy, there was certainly an *open* effort between the studios and the Roosevelt administration to influence the opinions of others "for predetermined ends" through manipulation.

Nonetheless, it is misleading to suggest that OWI succeeded in creating a new era in Hollywood filmmaking or in replacing the studios' old political and social assumptions with a new set of basic tenets. Indeed, Mellett and Poynter complained that the studios were only rarely adhering to OWI policies. When they attempted to increase their duties to include the supervision of finished scripts and films, the major studios reacted with an uproar. The headline in *Variety* the day after Mellett promised to step up film supervision was "CENSORS SHARPEN AXES;"[52] the heads of a number of studios protested to OWI chief Davis, who rapidly backed off from his assistant's proclamation. But what Mellett had proposed was no more than what a number of other organizations had done for years. The film industry's own office of censorship, the Production Code Administration, had the right to view and demand changes to finished films, as did the Catholic Church and several foreign governments. But the major studios were not willing to grant a federal agency such a degree of control over Hollywood films; Mayer and the Warner brothers, for example, both argued that they were loyally following the OWI policies anyway.[53]

The war brought an agency for propaganda to Hollywood, but that agency did not have more control over the studios than did the separate studio heads themselves. If MGM and Warner Brothers were going to change their implicit ideals of citizenship, those changes would have to come separately, from the studio moguls. They had pledged to change their stories, to provide audiences with pedagogical models of republican virtue in wartime, and with living (if fictional) propagandistic exempla who could clarify the reasons behind the sacrifices—of resources, of civil liberties, of alternate models of political engagement—demanded by the administration. The degree to which this happened, and to which the moguls turned to models that citizens could and should emulate, must be evaluated in the films themselves, not solely in the OWI manual. The proof, as Harry Warner told Senators Wheeler and Nye, "is in the pudding."[54]

No film better captures the repositioning of MGM's prewar ideal private citizen than *Mrs. Miniver* (1942), directed by William Wyler. The film's small English village is a transplanted version of Andy Hardy's American small town. The first twenty minutes of the film are devoted to Mrs. Miniver's (Greer Garson) attempt to tell her husband (Walter Pidgeon) that she has bought an expensive hat; the following fifteen minutes follow the circumstances of her son's crush on the granddaughter of a local land-owner. By the time the war enters the story, the Minivers and their town have been clearly defined within the context of the idyllic and apolitical hamlets that constituted the public world of prewar MGM America. As the scrolled introduction informs us, however, this "average middle class family . . . happy . . . easygoing . . . [and] careless" will presently be "fight-ing desperately for its way of life." The Minivers' son becomes a pilot, their village is repeatedly shelled, Mr. Miniver pilots a boat to Dunkirk to transport defeated British soldiers across the Channel, and a downed German pilot holds Mrs. Miniver at gunpoint.[55] After the police have taken the Nazi into custody, the Minivers discuss the event in the banter-ing tone in which they previously discussed ladies' hats, but the context of their situation has been completely transformed.

At the close of *Mrs. Miniver,* the residents of the small English town gather in their shelled church. The vicar exhorts his congregation (and the film's audience) to further exertions, situating all of them in the position now taken by the Minivers. There is no contradiction between the Mini-vers' position as typical middle-class people and their need to fight the Nazis. As the vicar makes clear in his sermon, it is precisely the Minivers' identity as an ideal MGM family that necessitates their heroism:

> This is not only a war of soldiers in uniform, it is a war of the people—of all the people—and it must be fought, not only on the battlefield, but in the cities and in the villages, in the factories and on the farms, in the home and in the heart of every man, woman, and child who loves freedom. Well, we have buried our dead but we shall not forget them. Instead, they will inspire us with an unbreakable determination to free ourselves and those who come after us from the tyranny and terror that threaten to strike us down. Fight it then! Fight it with all that is in us! And may God defend the right.

As "Onward Christian Soldiers" plays on the sound track, the townspeo-ple look up through the hole in the church roof at a squadron of English planes on its way to battle. The Minivers learn to reconcile their prewar existence and their need to throw themselves into the war effort. Gazing up reverently in church, the Minivers see combat planes; war heroes and war dead can be their models of heroism.[56] The Minivers' piety toward the Allied civil religion compels them in their capacity as an "average middle-class family" to take on heroic tasks.

As Mayer had expected his staff and his audience to walk in the steps of Andy Hardy's quintessential Americanism, so he expected them to rise to the demanding role of wartime citizens. As before, he intended to lead the way. Indeed, when Greer Garson exhibited reticence about playing the role of Mrs. Miniver, Mayer acted out the part for her, giving her the example (both as a patriot and as an actor trying to surpass "the best actor on the lot") that she had to emulate. Providing exempla of virtuous wartime citizens on- and offscreen (and fan magazines such as *Photoplay* collapsed stars and their roles, assuring readers of the actors' heroic support of the war effort), MGM personnel made war heroes available to audiences throughout the nation. Viewers could see Mrs. Miniver—Greer Garson—and other stars on film and at fund-raisers and rallies and take them as their models. Roosevelt apparently thought *Mrs. Miniver* would have such an exhortatory effect on audiences: he ordered that the film's closing sermon be printed on leaflets and dropped in occupied territories.[57]

It is significant, however, that the conflict in MGM's most inspirational war film is resolved by small-town piety. Replacing the thirst for glory with a sense of dutiful loyalty, Mayer attempts to contain emulatory ambition within the conservative world he trumpeted before the war. But the investment in essentialist hierarchy is not unique to Mayer, as Otis's and Harry and Jack Warner's fights against unionization—and, indeed, against any unauthorized public action—demonstrate. Even when the democratic pedagogue calls on his audience to eschew mimesis and strive with the models provided, in other words, the mimetic principle remains active. The audience member, whether colonized subject or member of the community, is subject to the principles of the project to mirror preexisting hierarchies and identities that Bhabha describes and Otis imported from the Spanish-American War to the faux Spanish paradise he and Harry Chandler refounded in the California desert. The mission of MGM's models, like that of Washington's new Romans and Otis's self-made citizenry, remained a profoundly conservative one.

MGM's films were not ideologically or narratively uniform, however.

Despite Mayer's formula and the demands of wartime mobilization, the studio's output was still less unified and directed than were Otis's models. The studio released period musicals, cartoons, and comedies that largely ignored the war. In some instances, MGM deviated from its small-town representation of the world at the request of OWI. *Thirty Seconds over Tokyo* (1944), for example, represents a favorite OWI theme, the merging of sharply defined individuals into dedicated combat teams. The heroic General Doolittle (Spencer Tracy), the brave but wary soldiers and sailors, and the American and Chinese operatives all coalesce around the need to defeat the enemy, seamlessly combining their characters into a larger cause—a shift that one or two years previously would have required lengthy exposition. A new body politic replaces the homogeneous and passive communities of 1930s MGM here, one that is active, heterogeneous, and ideologically motivated. Indeed, some wartime communities resembled the Popular Front more closely than they resembled Carvel. The platoon film was popular throughout the war, reassuring audiences that combat was capable of extending the communities of prewar MGM to all people. More characteristic of the MGM style is *Song of Russia* (1943), an attempt to transport *Mrs. Miniver* to the Soviet Union. Robert Taylor plays an American composer who falls in love with a Russian pianist; the two visit a Soviet "collective," which is indistinguishable from an American small-town farm, get married in a Russian Orthodox church, and honeymoon in the United States after the Nazi invasion.

Warner Brothers also adapted to the forms and topics of the war. In a Cary Grant vehicle about the war in the Pacific, *Destination Tokyo* (1943), director Delmer Daves used a funeral oration to exhort audiences to wartime virtue.[58] At the funeral for a popular chief petty officer who was stabbed by a Japanese prisoner, Grant offers the Roosevelt administration line for why Hollywood needs to provide the right models as he outlines the results of enemy pedagogy: while American children get roller skates for Christmas, he tells us, Japanese children are taught to play with knives. "Mike died to put an end to a system that puts knives in the hands of young children. If Mike was here, I think he'd say that was what he'd died for—to put more roller skates in the hands of kids, even the next generation of Japanese kids." Like roller skates at Christmas, American culture and the pedagogical models it produces could be disseminated to wider audiences, teaching civic virtue, Hollywood-style.

Directed by *Angels with Dirty Faces'* Michael Curtiz, *Casablanca* (1942) perfectly demonstrates the transition from the standard Warner Brothers heroes of the 1930s to the Warner Brothers war heroes, emulable figures who are converted from flawed private existences to the civic virtue of wartime conditions. Bogart once again plays the quintessential solitary hero of questionable legal standing, similar to the heroes that Warner Brothers specialized in throughout the Depression. Bogart's Rick Blaine functions as the bridge between the private American solitary tough-guy hero of the studio's prewar films and the emulable public war hero of the 1940s by illustrating a shortcoming in the heroic character that prewar Warner Brothers associated with American virtue. In order to be truly heroic now, Americans would need to do more than endure; they would have to follow models of war heroism. *Casablanca,* like *Mrs. Miniver,* challenges audiences to act in the manner of heroic models, to strive and sacrifice and potentially emulate the film's heroes.

"It's December 1941 in Casablanca," a mournful Rick says to his piano player, Sam. "What time is it in New York? . . . I bet they're asleep in New York. I bet they're asleep all over America." But as Sam points out, their

Rick (Humphrey Bogart) alone in *Casablanca* (1942).

"watches have stopped"; everyone in America is awake *as of* December 1941, and the time has come for Rick to wake up too. In this regard, it is useful to contrast him with the film's other heroic figure, Resistance leader Victor Laszlo. Laszlo provides a moral center for those who oppose the Nazis, and the Germans want to kill him because of his exemplary influence. When Laszlo leads the crowd at Rick's Café Americain in drowning out the Germans' chorus of "Die Wacht am Rhein" with their own singing of "La Marseillaise," for example, Nazi Major Heinrich Strasser complains, "If Laszlo's presence in a café can inspire this unfortunate demonstration, what more can his presence in Casablanca bring on?" But Laszlo's position as a moral exemplar actually removes him from the emulable world of the Hollywood movies; he is *so* good, such a figure of moral certitude, that he fails to reflect the ambivalence of the studios or their target audience. It is Rick, who starts from a position of isolation and is slowly convinced to engage in global politics, who represents the emulable Hollywood hero. Rick has joined the larger struggle, but he has not abandoned the private and personal position from which he (and the other Hollywood heroes) started. As Dana Polan writes, Rick's story is taking

Rick with Ilsa (Ingrid Bergman).

place in a "kind of atopia, a space outside the official representation of struggle," and even after he joins the war effort he still stands outside the military world.[59] Bridging the isolated heroism of Warner Brothers 1930s movies and the commitment to combined struggle of the typical war films, *Casablanca* represents the Hollywood studios' work to transform twenty years' worth of imitable but unchallenging individuated models into an emulatory struggle for active wartime citizenship. The transformation was not an ideological shift—studio output was still premised on a promise of mimetic accuracy, reminding audiences of virtues they ostensibly possessed—but even at this level, the Southern California media were again serving the purposes of mobilizing American narratives in the service of virtuous warfare.

The Popular Front and other politically active members of the Hollywood creative community, meanwhile, were increasingly active in prowar projects outside of their films. For the duration of the war, film personnel from Republican mogul Louis B. Mayer to Communist screenwriter John Howard Lawson could align around some basic concepts of American

Rick returns to the fight. Although he is now allied with Louis, he still looks away, a solitary figure.

civic ideals. Throughout the early 1940s, while moguls helped to craft films urging audiences to emulate Mrs. Miniver's and Rick Blaine's conversion to larger public commitments, left-wing directors, actors, and screenwriters could work for political causes on- and offscreen that five years previously would have endangered their contracts. The shift to emulation and politicization reflects a shared belief in the crisis faced by the United States. Otis had intended to use emulation and the colonial forms of mimicry he learned in the Spanish-American War to redeem the nation from "industrial slavery"; now Mayer, the Warner brothers, and others were attempting to use emulation and film heroics to save American political virtues from foreign attack.

In many cases, the work produced by members of the Popular Front was far from radical; invoking many of the same political icons as the moguls, Hollywood leftists differed only in their emphases. As Ceplair and Englund point out, the Hollywood left "shared their conservative opponents' ideological underpinnings: loyalty to, and faith in, the American democratic tradition and its possibilities; the importance of American nationality in defining a person; the commitment to 'liberty' as represented by the various founding documents of the American Republic."[60] Where Mayer's 1930s films may have invoked American founders to legitimate the imitation of his ideal small-town world, screenwriters such as Dalton Trumbo invoked different aspects of the same models (the American founders' "revolutionary" legacy, for example) to encourage audiences toward more active political strategies. During the war the invocation of an emulatory attitude toward antifascist heroes became standard within the industry, and even James K. McGuinness, a reactionary writer and producer, would later testify that he "could find no fault with the performance of radicals during World War II, especially with the content of their scripts." "During that time," McGuinness testified, "under my general supervision Dalton Trumbo wrote two magnificent patriotic scripts, *A Guy Named Joe,* and *Thirty Seconds over Tokyo.*"[61] For their part, the Hollywood radicals "had no difficulty," in the words of Ceplair and Englund, "accepting . . . affirmations of faith in 'the democratic process' and 'the deepening and strengthening of democracy.' . . . The Communists were always quoting Jefferson and Paine, using, [screenwriter Phillip] Dunne recalled, the short form of their first names—Tom—only."[62]

The attempt of conservatives and radicals alike to cite historical patriotic models underscores the profound democratic search for stasis and author-ity in even the emulatory challenges of wartime film. As we have seen, Arendt traces the word "authority" to the Latin root *augere*, the augmen-tation of the work of the founding. Our would-be exempla—Otis, the moguls, even the Hollywood radicals—are attempting to ground their authority in light of their own chosen founders (even when they pose as founders in their own right). Emulation demands striving with a model, of course, but it requires a model to begin with—for democratic learning to take place, these actors insist, we must first reinscribe and reinforce our schoolmasters. Congressional opponents of the Roosevelt administration, however, posited that the moguls were actually attempting to undermine the Republic that Mayer and the Warner brothers purported to mirror.

When the House Un-American Activities Committee was created in 1934, it was intended to be part of the antifascist movement.[63] HUAC was created in part to investigate pro-Nazi "fifth column" activities. By the end of the decade, however, the chairmanship of HUAC had fallen to Repre-sentative Martin Dies, an anti-Semitic Texas Democrat, and the commit-tee's target changed.[64] In 1939, Dies took his committee to Hollywood and began investigating reports from members of the American Legion that the Communist Party was using Popular Front organizations, including the Hollywood Anti-Nazi League, to gain influence over American movies. He established residence in a hotel in Hollywood and summoned many members of the film community who had been accused of membership in subversive organizations. The investigations led nowhere; Dies left Holly-wood pronouncing that he had found no evidence of subversion. The Senate War Propaganda Subcommittee was next to investigate conspiracy in Hollywood, but it too had no real effect on the political life of the film community.[65]

Even before the war was over, the right-wing Motion Picture Alliance for the Preservation of American Ideals began calling on HUAC to re-turn.[66] When committee chair John Rankin, a Republican from Missis-sippi, and his investigators finally did come to Hollywood to engage in a preliminary investigation in the summer of 1947, the Alliance provided them with a large list of suspected Communist agents.[67] Among the peo-ple HUAC subpoenaed was Jack Warner. The mogul's tough individual-ist persona crumbled before the committee when his ally was no longer Roosevelt, but, rather, a group of writers and labor activists he had battled in the 1930s. Warner provided the committee with the names of his own employees whom he suspected of Communist loyalties, and his list included virtually every politically active liberal and radical of the previous fifteen years.

During the early 1940s, the political icons invoked by leftists and moguls alike were the same; the change Hollywood had made was in exhorting viewers to strive with those icons somewhat. But that level of political engagement was too much for HUAC's definition of citizenship, one that assumed a greater degree of passivity than that found among Otis's foot soldiers or the citizens of Carvel. Imitation, according to HUAC and its supporters, was likely to be an *unconscious* process in the minds of essentially malleable citizens. Before the war, right-wing isolationists in the Congress had accused the film moguls of conspiring to force the United States into a war. Now that the battle against fascism had been supplanted by the Cold War, HUAC was using the war films against the Hollywood studios, branding them as examples of the sort of active political effort that the committee defined as subversive.[68]

HUAC began hearings in October 1947, subpoenaing forty-three members of the film community, twenty-four of whom were Alliance members and "friendly witnesses." The moguls themselves turned their backs on their wartime activist allies. In doing so, they were falling back on the basic models of American citizenship they had always celebrated. The Warner brothers would bend to what they now perceived to be a patriotic duty, provided it did not cost them control over their studio. Louis B. Mayer resisted HUAC's attempts to assert control over his bully pulpit but was otherwise supportive of the committee's hostility toward the politics of the wartime Roosevelt administration. The Warner brothers and Mayer argued that Hollywood did have a problem with Communist subversion, but that the Communists had no effect on the studios' film output. They promised, therefore, to cooperate with HUAC but insisted they did not need government assistance in freeing themselves of Red influence. They were, in short, willing to subscribe to the committee's view that the nation was in a new political crisis and was threatened by radical subversion, provided that they could withdraw to the ideal "nations" that their studios had depicted before the war.

The "Hollywood Ten," HUAC witnesses who refused to cooperate or to recognize the constitutional legitimacy of the committee, were held in contempt of Congress and sentenced to prison.[69] The studio moguls, wary of trouble from Washington, fired the Ten for violating the "morals clauses" in their studio contracts. Once the moguls caved in to demands that the Ten be fired, the precedent of the "blacklist" was set. As the Ten were fired for violating morals clauses, any studio employee held in contempt could be fired, even if he or she did not serve jail time. As time passed, any member of the film community suspected of subversion was susceptible to "blacklisting."

A number of members of the Popular Front, meanwhile, joined forces to attack HUAC and its methods publicly. Humphrey Bogart and Lauren Bacall, Kirk Douglas, Katharine Hepburn, John Garfield, Edward G. Robinson, Gene Kelly, and others, calling themselves the Committee for the First Amendment, flew to Washington; in the light of publicity, the CFA intended to keep alive the political activism they had demonstrated in their films.[70] The activism of the CFA, however, was itself premised on the democratic *augere* of the U.S. Constitution—looking back to 1789 for their models, the Hollywood radicals were, in fact, reinforcing the state apparatus that was being turned against them. HUAC, part of the postwar complex of expanding security bureaucracies, only benefited from the patriotic zeal of the film community, and Bogart and the others eventually performed acts of mimetic consent at the direction of the House countersubversives.[71] Indeed, Bogart, who had represented the archetypal individualist war hero of the early 1940s, recanted his role in the CFA and in many of the leading liberal organizations of wartime Hollywood. Having been warned by Ed Sullivan that "the public is beginning to think you're a Red!" Bogart published an article in *Photoplay* ("I'm No Communist") claiming that he had been "a dope," tricked into supporting subversive causes. As Rick Blaine had eased the transition from individualist to patriotic hero, Bogart led the way in what was to become a public ritual of confession and contrition.[72]

In 1951, HUAC issued 110 more subpoenas. The majority of the witnesses called followed a strict model of behavior, admitting to guilt or youthful folly, applauding the efforts of the committee, and naming other individuals they had known while working in "subversive" organizations. The ritual called into question every liberal organization and cause of the previous decade, including domestic efforts to battle fascism. The narrative with which HUAC coached witnesses posited two ideas: that the committee was vital for the preservation of civic virtue in the United States, and that the civic virtue for which it fought precluded any independent and potentially unauthorized political activity.

Rather than eschewing political imitation, HUAC developed a model of its own. As Otis and the Merchants and Manufacturers' Association had proffered the models of defeated subjects and loyal foot soldiers, HUAC now proffered a model of repentance that was methodically rehearsed. Mendel Silberberg, an entertainment attorney with a close relationship to many of the studio moguls, organized the Community Relations Council. The CRC, in Gabler's phrase, "brokered" deals among members of the film community who were charged with subversive activity, their accusers, and the studio heads. CRC executive director Joseph Roos and Martin Gang, another successful entertainment lawyer, were soon training witnesses to give testimony, guiding them through the process of public recitation, confession, and accusation that HUAC required of them.[73]

When HUAC and the CRC engaged in mimesis, they provided even more hierarchical control than Otis had. Screenwriter Bess Taffel, explaining her decision to take the Fifth Amendment when appearing in Washington, said:

> I was unwilling to perjure myself as, I was convinced, the cooperative witnesses were doing. The pattern of their testimony bore out my feeling that they were repeating scenarios given to them, providing expected responses involving self-denigration, the admission of having been duped, the spewing out of anti-Communist sentiments, and, of course, the lists to be named.[74]

A handful of witnesses were allowed to wander from the provided script; Lucille Ball, for example, essentially played a variation of her popular "scatterbrained" public role, admitting to having registered as a Communist in the early 1930s to please her grandfather but assuring the committee that she had not understood the situation and that she had not voted. For most of the witnesses, however, atoning for any time spent in liberal political activity, and particularly in the activity of exhorting moviegoers to political struggle (even after the fashion of cinematic war heroes), required an act of mimetic surrender.[75]

In fact, the committee held the act of exhorting audiences to action in particular contempt. Wary of the use of cinematic models to spur citizens to action, members of HUAC had little doubt that film was a power-ful tool for shaping opinion. Rather than the relationship envisioned by Otis or Mayer, however, the HUAC members believed that citizens were impelled to action by hidden messages. John Rankin, expanding on Nye's original argument, claimed that Jews and Communists in Hollywood had undertaken a plan to spread "un-American propaganda, as well as their loathsome, lying, immoral, anti-Christian filth before the eyes of your children in every community in America."[76] According to Rankin and fel-low committee member J. Parnell Thomas, a Democrat from New Jersey, the Hollywood left had been inserting propagandistic messages into the entertainment medium, using film to cast doubt on American institutions and to spread faith in Communist principles.[77] Members of HUAC had very little faith in the conscious striving with one's models that is endemic to emulatory *virtú*, but they had a profound belief in the ability of hidden messages to brainwash a simplistic citizenry.

It is useful, at this point, to return briefly to the studios' film output. *White Heat*, a 1949 Warner Brothers film, provides a striking contrast with wartime and even prewar movies. In this film, directed by Raoul Walsh, James Cagney returns to the gangster roles that he eschewed during the war. Cody Jarrett, Cagney's character, bears some resemblance to Rocky Sullivan and other 1930s outlaw heroes, following an illegal self-made-man model and nursing the ambition to reach the "top of the world." In the postwar world, however, the context has changed. Jarrett is a criminal because he is mentally unbalanced and morbidly attached to his mother; his foe is not a rival heroic figure, but a monolithic governmental agency. At the film's end, Jarrett stands atop a large spherical oil drum, bellowing, "Top of the world, Ma!" when an FBI sharpshooter succeeds in igniting the drum. In the original shooting script, another FBI agent then sneers, "'Top of the world' . . . why do they even try?" The heroic individualism of wartime Warner Brothers had been pushed back further into passivity and futility than it had been before the war.

White Heat was not as typical of Warner Brothers films as *The Public Enemy* or *Angels with Dirty Faces* had been. Indeed, no film could be. By the mid-1950s, the studio system of the prewar years and the degree of genre conformity it was able to ensure were gone for good. The enforced dives-titure of the studios' distribution system rendered the mass production

The classical pose: Representative John Rankin in a toga made of pro-HUAC petitions. Reprinted with permission from AP/Wide World Photos.

of B-movie series like the Andy Hardy films and most gangster movies unprofitable. Meanwhile, the rapid growth of independent production companies, the division of the national bloc of movie audiences, and the advent of television undercut the creation of cohesive social exempla tied to specific studios. The men who created the exempla were soon gone as well. Mayer was forced out of the MGM presidency when Loew's attempted to bring in someone who could adapt the studio's films to compete with television.[78] Harry and Jack Warner sold their interests in their studio, so embittered by long-term rivalries that they never spoke to each other again. In the aftermath of Hollywood's failed attempts to inhabit a *virtuoso* public space, the prewar imitable genres of citizenship and virtue were swept away along with the powerful moguls who created them.

The ideal Hollywood audience member was static and saw in film exempla only larger-than-life versions of him- or herself. In the case of MGM's model, the nation is suffused with latent virtue. No one need worry about surpassing the fame of an exalted exemplar; the ideal citizen, according to Mayer, must only recognize and live up to his or her part in that exemplary society (as Andy Hardy accepts his birthright or as Dorothy Gale learns to embrace Kansas). At Warner Brothers, the tough individual does not try to change the world, but rather strives to endure it without breaking. As Nick Roddick points out, even during the exhoratory 1940s, "the message [of American film] is that the individual owes society a complete commitment to ensuring that it can continue on its established course."[79] And despite the apparent division between the reassuring conservativism of the most radical of Hollywood actors and the visionary demands of, for example, "Tom" Paine, it is precisely this mimetic privileging of the status quo that we find throughout our models of emulatory challenges; even demands for a radical democratic pedagogy bring us back to the static dimensions of mimetic politics.

Faith in the necessity of political imitation remained an important factor in Los Angeles throughout the 1950s, however. The most influential proponent of political imitation and emulation in 1950s Los Angeles was a figure from the right wing of Southern California politics, but not the materialistic right wing of Harry Chandler. He was a zealot for reactionary politics who excoriated corrupt politicians such as J. Parnell Thomas, a paranoiac lawman who was feared and despised by J. Edgar Hoover. He used the new medium of television to spread his model before a national public, but, unlike the studio moguls, he demanded that his audience live up to and compete with his ideals. He exhorted emulation from the citizens of Los Angeles, and his attempt to elicit that behavior continues to affect the political and economic existence of Southern California. Police Chief William Parker was the most passionate defender of the concept of emulation that Southern California has ever produced, and his long career provides us with the most vivid image on record of the failure of emulation for political life.

THE BADGE

William Parker, Daryl Gates,
and the LAPD

The liberty of men is never assured by the institutions and laws that are intended to guarantee them. . . . Not because they are ambiguous, but simply because "liberty" is what must be exercised.

—MICHEL FOUCAULT

If it takes one blow . . . or if it takes eight thousand blows to overcome resistance, then that's what it takes.

—CHARLES DUKE, LAPD

"This," Jack Webb intoned at the beginning of every episode of one of the highest-rated shows on early television, "is the city. Los Angeles, California." Like Harry Warner only a decade before, Webb promised perfect mimetic representation. Webb's imitation was explicitly wedded to another grandiose attempt at refounding Los Angeles and, indeed, at reminding the nation as a whole of its original defining principles in order to mobilize it for the demands of another global war. Machiavelli wrote that republics should be brought back to their "original principles" to keep them from growing corrupt. The example of particularly virtuous citizens would be important in such a moment of rebirth, because of their ability to inspire or shame others into imitating their example.[1] When William Parker became chief of police of Los Angeles in 1950, he argued that the

Los Angeles Police Department must provide an exemplar of this sort and that Angelenos must emulate that exemplar. The growth of government and business in Southern California during World War II and afterward presented, in Parker's opinion, a potent threat to Los Angeles and the American Republic. Los Angeles's only hope of avoiding corruption was the citizenry's active emulation of a model of civic virtue. By the time of his death in 1966, however, Parker had grown embittered by the failure of Angelenos to follow his lead. For the following three decades, the leadership of the LAPD strove to preserve the post-Watts remnants of Parker's legacy, coupling his faith in the exemplary nature of Los Angeles' police officers with his ultimate contempt for the citizens of Los Angeles.

From the turn of the century until 1950, the Los Angeles Police Department was a fairly typical metropolitan police force of its era. By current

"How to protect your home": Chief James Edgar Davis and family. Photograph courtesy of University of Southern California, on behalf of the U.S.C. Specialized Libraries and Archival Collections.

standards, it was corrupt: there was a system of payoffs from certain large criminal enterprises, and some policemen reportedly traded cash for promotions.[2] Acts of racially motivated police brutality were not uncommon; the "zoot suit riots" and the Sleepy Lagoon murder trial are only the most famous of police attacks on Los Angeles minority communities.[3]

In the late 1930s, Harry Raymond, a private detective and former police chief of Venice and San Diego, was hired by CIVIC (the Citizens Independent Vice Investigating Committee), a Progressive watchdog organization, to investigate police corruption in Los Angeles. In January 1938, Raymond was almost killed by a bomb that had been connected to his car's ignition. Three months later, the head of the LAPD's Special Intelligence Division was convicted of planting the car bomb. A Progressive candidate, Fletcher Bowron, was elected mayor, and the police department was reorganized. The intelligence unit was disbanded and twenty-three high-ranking LAPD officers were forced to resign, but smaller scandals continued to plague the police department. Finally, in 1950, the Police Commission appointed as chief a reform-minded twenty-three-year LAPD veteran, a former altar boy with a reputation for probity, William H. Parker. A committed agent of reform who transformed and strengthened the LAPD's coercive arsenal of racist and antipolitical strategies, Parker provides us with a vivid picture of the damage mimetic hierarchies have inflicted on the political culture of Los Angeles.

Parker was born in Lead, in the Black Hills of South Dakota. His grandfather had been a peace officer in Lead years before, and the "Wild West lawman" image held some fascination for Parker and several reporters, as well as for Parker's biographers in later years.[4] He joined the LAPD in the late 1920s and worked as a patrolman while pursuing his law degree. By the time he graduated, the country was in the Great Depression, and he chose to stay with the relative security of his job in the LAPD. Early in his career he established a reputation for ardently following departmental rules and regulations, and when Bowron became mayor he was in no fear of losing his position. Parker left the LAPD only once: during World War II he helped create new police departments in occupied Germany. Thus Parker, like Otis, trained in imposing American models of surrender on conquered subjects before carrying out domestic exemplary wars.

After his return to Los Angeles, Parker took charge of the new Internal Affairs Division, investigating criminal complaints against Los Angeles

Police Department officers. He was holding that position when he became chief. Parker came to his new office with a passionate dedication to police reform. In his opinion, Los Angeles had the capacity to be an exemplar to other cities throughout the nation of the sort of moral existence that he felt the Republic required. To this end, he wished to remove the police department from what he felt were the corrupting effects of politics. As Otis had required military order before he could create his autonomous city of self-made men, Parker wanted his exemplar to be free of partisan fighting so that it could remain true to the ideals that were necessary for the rebirth of American virtue. In the mid-1930s, Parker had placed a provision on the ballot that made it very difficult for the city to fire policemen and impossible to fire the police chief without a long series of public hearings, and in 1950 he intended to use that law to create and maintain the police force that he wanted. The Police Commission was all but reduced to figurehead status, and Parker's position became unassailable. He also moved to set police salaries at a fixed percentage of the city budget.[5] Safe from the need to haggle with other civic elites, Parker felt secure enough to begin a career as an exemplar, a figure that the citizens of Los Angeles would need to learn to emulate.

This schoolmaster, however, promised a set of radical revisions. In his policies and his public pronouncements, William Parker was extremely forthright about his vision for the Los Angeles Police Department.[6] In speeches he made in the 1950s, he defined his vision of the LAPD's role, a vision of an elite corps that would control crime but, more important, provide the citizens of Los Angeles with a model of civic excellence that they could emulate—indeed, that they would have to emulate.

In several speeches presented during the early 1950s, Parker outlined his agenda for the "new" LAPD:

> We're disappointing Washington and the other Founders. By disassociating Virtue from our search for prosperity, we threaten to follow the course of Babylon, Rome, etc. We need a great moral leader to pull us from the brink.[7]

As this quotation suggests, Parker was not a traditional booster of Los Angeles. In his opinion, the city was already so morally compromised that it stood on the brink of spiritual and political collapse, yet it still had the opportunity to be saved by an active and virtuous citizenry. He saw the central task of his LAPD to be the political education of that citizenry, in a fashion similar to that set forth by Machiavelli in his *Discourses:* "These men are of such reputation and their example is so powerful that good men wish to imitate them, and the wicked are ashamed to live a life contrary to theirs."[8] Otis had used his political and economic resources and his experience in the Philippines to refound Los Angeles as a uniquely American metropolis. Parker, too, wanted to mobilize media, money, and influence for the purpose of a colonial reshaping of the citizens of L.A., but, in the chief's telling, Southern California was already well past founding moments and deep into a period of corruption and decay.

Parker saw the mission of his police department in very broad terms. Crime, as he defined it, was only the outward result of an inner sickness that had already made Los Angeles a dark and dangerous city and that threatened the rest of the American Republic as well. Thus it would be

William Parker sworn in as chief of police, 1951. Courtesy of Herald-Examiner Collection, Los Angeles Public Library 00044647.

irresponsible of the LAPD to spend its time merely trying to catch criminals. He asserted: "It is imperative that every American recognize crime, not as a police problem, but as a departure from the deep convictions that bind 150 million persons into a secure, happy nation. The police must help them understand" by publicly displaying "ethics and morality."[9] "The first requirement in the performance" of police work, Parker told the 1951 Police Academy graduating class, "is that we policemen be both moral and honest."[10] Completing this task required an active effort on the part of the citizens of Los Angeles to equal and even exceed the LAPD in ethics and morality as, "largely by his political ethics, the citizen determines the ethics of the police."[11] Without this emulatory partnership of police and citizens, Los Angeles and the nation as a whole were destined to follow in the footsteps of bad models, such as Babylon, Rome, and other ancient civilizations whose "walls crumbled" when *"barbarism* within rotted the moral supporting timbers."[12] Like Roman citizens and their exempla of virtue, the LAPD and the other citizens of Los Angeles would create virtue in their city and their nation by striving with each other's models, "outvying" each other in their attempt to forestall corruption and create glory.

The role that the LAPD played for Los Angeles, Los Angeles would then play for the nation.

> There are those of us who sincerely believe that this nation must undergo a moral and spiritual rebirth if it is to survive. . . . Most everything that happens in LA is scrutinized throughout the nation. It is fitting, therefore, that we should set the pattern for a complete return to fundamental honesty in government, in business, and in our daily lives.[13]

Once great moral leadership was achieved, the battle could be joined. Much depended, in Parker's argument, on "ordinary citizens." He worked quickly to establish policies to aid those citizens in living up to the model set by his police department.

Parker's first policy reforms as chief were aimed at the Police Academy. The Academy became more selective in the people it admitted. Entrance examinations became more difficult, and high school and college graduates soon made up a larger percentage of the force. Parker instituted a height requirement of five feet, nine inches, the average height for American men in 1950, so that his police officers would be less likely to have to look up when speaking with civilians.[14] The Academy training facility was patterned on a military boot camp, and Parker hired a large number of former U.S. Army and Marine Corps drill instructors to train his personnel. Indeed, a ten-point bonus was granted to the civil service ranking of any LAPD officer who had previously served in the military.[15]

Parker also initiated a practice that Chief Daryl Gates would later term "proactive policing." The officers of the LAPD had to concern themselves with Parker's "big picture" of crime. Because, according to that view, illegal activities arose from civic corruption and fueled that corruption in turn, police officers who waited until a crime had been committed before moving into action (as did officers in other police departments throughout the nation) would be behaving irresponsibly. LAPD officers would need to act *before* a crime was committed to do their jobs effectively. In Gates's words, "If someone looked out of place in a neighborhood, we had a little chat with him."[16] Anyone suspicious could be questioned in an

William Parker inspects police academy graduates, 1966. Courtesy of Herald-Examiner Collection, Los Angeles Public Library 00044653.

attempt to preempt crime. Proactive policing was a civic duty in Parker's eyes. Police policy was being set to solve crimes, but also to provide a moral environment in which citizens could battle "the barbarism within."

Proactive policing also enabled the LAPD to map the city, providing various models and styles of coercion to different communities according to Parker's standard of educability. In chapter 1, we saw how Otis employed emulatory rhetoric and the imitative mode I compared with Bhabha's colonial mimicry, a disciplinary strategy to create "a reformed, recognizable Other, as a subject of difference that is almost the same, but not quite."[17] Parker employed African American clergy to provide such a model for the virtues he defined as intrinsic to blacks in Southern California. He also resisted attempts to unite L.A.'s black and white communities. Proactive policing provided a rationale for closing successful jazz clubs and record stores on Los Angeles' Central Avenue, as, Parker argued, racial integration could instigate class violence as well as provide a dangerous combination of incompatible civic exempla.[18]

To ensure proper surveillance of such "barbarism," Parker reinstituted and modernized the Police Department Intelligence Division, which had been dissolved after the attempt on Harry Raymond's life. Parker's PDID fought a two-front war against possible sources of corruption. The section devoted to intelligence on organized crime developed a nationwide intelligence organization, compiling files on known gangsters from around the country.[19] Officers were stationed at Southern California airports with complete files, and anyone suspected of mob activity who landed in L.A. was immediately detained and put on a departing plane. Here, too, Parker drew on his experience as part of a successful military occupation. As Webb describes it, the proactive "approach, based on the military G-2 system, meant that investigations got underway *before* the violence erupted. . . . LAPD's Intelligence men . . . followed the individual, rather than the crime."[20]

The other arm of the PDID was assigned to the compilation of political intelligence. In Parker's view, crime and political subversion were intricately connected forms of corruption, and the only way to detect larger patterns of such civic decay was to amass the most public material possible.[21] Records were kept of all public meetings and political speeches; officers were detailed to keep political figures under surveillance; journals and newspapers were combed for possible clues to spreading barbarism. Within ten years, Parker's intelligence organization was operating nationally, occasionally in competition with J. Edgar Hoover's Federal Bureau of Investigation. In addition to aiding the LAPD in the proactive elimination of deviant behavior from the city, the intelligence files (which were classified as "The Property of the Chief: Not Subject to Subpoena") also served as political insurance against competing elites whose indiscretions might have been recorded by the PDID. As Otis had done before him, Parker was establishing control over anyone who might question his definition of the ideal Los Angeles.

Such covert activities were part of Parker's overall vision, a defensive strategy to keep Los Angeles pure until the citizenry was strong enough to recognize barbarism on its own. Intelligence activities, by definition a secret from the majority of Angelenos, could not spur the local population to virtuous action, however. To further his emulatory purpose, Parker created the Public Information Division. In 1956, under the direction of Stanley Sheldon, the officers of the PID were assigned to maintain open and friendly relations with local news organizations and media outlets. Summations of crime reports were prepared; officers were detailed not only to the *Los Angeles Times* but also to ethnic newspapers like *La Opinión* and the *Record*. They wrote stories that they sent to more than 150 newspapers throughout Southern California and clipped stories from papers (for themselves and the PDID). They organized public appearances for police officers and the police band.

Parker and his PID thus learned the lesson of OSS and the studio moguls before them—that political education and mobilization in a hierarchically organized democratic state is served by mass media, and that Hollywood could provide audiences for what Koppes and Black have termed a "unified field" in which the models of patriot and subversive, hero and villain, citizen and foreigner, could be represented repeatedly.[22] The PID produced "The Thin Blue Line," a question-and-answer television show featuring Chief Parker. The show was broadcast from a special set, an exact replica of Parker's office at police headquarters, with identical furniture and photos in the "windows" that showed the view from Parker's actual office. The goal of scrupulous aesthetic replication guided all of Parker's relations with television, as the studio moguls claimed it had with many of their films. The mass media would mimic the LAPD—any deviation would mar the carefully crafted exemplar that Parker was presenting—so that the audience could emulate the force.

Despite the fact that Parker was hoping to defend the nation against barbarism, he wanted to do more through political imitation than merely preserve the legacy of his ancestors. He hoped to create a city of virtue and moral strength, one that could prepare Americans for the struggle to achieve historic glory and fame through a Cold War victory over Communism. As he had exported his police methods to Germany after World War II, the United States would one day spread the example of its political and economic systems on a level that would surpass the corrupt models of antiquity and vanquish our Cold War foes.[23] This degree of ambition seems incongruous with the Hollywood mode of imitation. The absolute replication of what Harry Warner called "the world as it is" reinforced the conservative passivity inherent in a political culture premised on imitation rather than the zealous attempt to reshape the nation's citizens that Otis and Parker professed. Parker, however, used aesthetics as an aid to emulation. This combination provided the conceptual framework of the LAPD's most successful foray into popular culture.

Parker and the PID were extensively involved in the production of the second-highest-rated show (after *I Love Lucy*) on early-1950s television: Jack Webb's *Dragnet.* Webb's Sergeant Joe Friday became identified in the minds of the nation with Parker's vision of the LAPD. Friday was extremely efficient without being inhuman. A model of civic excellence, Joe was the sort of citizen Parker argued viewers should be like in whatever walk of life they occupied. Often pictured chatting with bartenders or fry cooks, Friday could also quote whole sections of the LAPD codebook from memory. Indeed, each episode of the show was presented as a police report come to life: Friday's monotone narration specified the dates, times, and locations of scenes and the specific crimes being committed and investigated. The opening of each episode featured shots of real locations around Los Angeles while Friday, in voice-over, provided statistical and historical information, summing up with a matter-of-fact connection to his role as professional policeman.[24] Parker provided Webb with the details of his vision; with mimetic perfection, Webb provided the audience with those details. At this point, emulation could enter the picture;

Joe Friday could be the model of civic excellence that the audience, just like victims on the show, could strive to equal or exceed.

Within the show's dialogue, Friday maintained his narrator status. The majority of his dialogue was terse; he often spoke in incomplete sentences, and only to derive necessary information. In almost all the episodes, Friday forces victims to calm down, to speak as he does, and to provide "just the facts." The pattern was uniform: a shaken victim would begin by providing vast amounts of information, and Friday would frequently interrupt with reminders to return to bare-bones exposition (e.g., "Yes, ma'am, but did you notice the color of the vehicle?").[25] The victim would usually stop to light a cigarette and then resume talking in Friday's monotone narrative style. Only witnesses and bystanders would break the dialogue's style, providing long and tiresome stories or complaints that would serve as the show's comedy relief.

Just as Friday provides only factual data for the audience, Webb wants to assure us that there is no fantasy involved in the format of *Dragnet*.

Sergeant Joe Friday (Jack Webb) and Officer Frank Smith (Ben Alexander) on the job: coffee and shotguns (*Dragnet*, 1954).

Indeed, Webb's first words in his narration are, "This is the city." As Hollywood had promised to use imitation to show "the way the world is," Webb employed his mimetic zeal to assure that his representation of Parker's ideal world showed "the way Los Angeles is." Each episode begins with a dry voice-over: "Ladies and gentlemen. The story you are about to see is true. The names have been changed to protect the innocent." At the end of each episode, the outside narrator's voice returns to state the date and outcome of the trial. Webb's thirst for veracity matched if not exceeded that of the PID. *Dragnet* sets were exact replicas of LAPD offices and L.A. locations, and each episode was supervised by PID liaisons.[26]

Although he was originally suspicious of the show, which was designed to spread the message of his LAPD without actually being within its bureaucracy, Parker maintained a close relationship with the production, and the Office of the Chief reviewed every script before shooting began. Indeed, unlike other TV shows, *Dragnet* did not close with a visual for the production company in charge (Webb's Mark VII Limited). The Mark VII Limited logo was the penultimate shot of every episode; the final shot was a picture of Friday's badge with the following words superimposed

A pulp image as moral exemplar (*Dragnet,* episode first aired September 2, 1953).

over it: "Technical advice for the filming of *Dragnet* came from the office of Chief W. H. Parker, LAPD." Webb's desire for complete accuracy meshed perfectly with Parker's vision of the proper relationship between the LAPD and television: perfect mimesis was a necessity to civic virtue and civil order, on television as well as in the streets.

Dragnet was not merely an artless summation of police procedures, however; it would not have cornered a regular audience of more than thirteen million homes within its first season if it had been.[27] Webb followed several popular film styles, including many conventions of the genre now known as film noir. Most of the stories were suspenseful, and despite Webb's sanguine vision of the LAPD, his general picture of Los Angeles was of a metropolis that was unstable, chaotic, and impersonal (if not hostile). Whereas most film noir movies of the 1940s presented individuals as dwarfed by the anarchic world around them, Webb used the same atmosphere to keep the exemplary Friday within a human scale. Despite his efficiency, Friday was capable of being frustrated or displaying humor, and the audience watched as he and his partner, Frank Smith, sat through pointless stakeouts or wolfed down greasy diner breakfasts and, on some occasions, as they failed to solve certain cases.[28] Webb shared the film moguls' concern about portraying human characters with whom his audience could identify; Friday's accomplishments were considerable, but they were within the grasp of the ordinary "Joes" who made up the majority of *Dragnet's* audience.

These elements of the show (the Hollywood B-movie professionalism and the "human" side of Friday) are brought to the fore in an early episode that concerns the first time Friday kills a suspect. The episode's story line, in which drug addicts are calling doctors to hotel rooms, beating them unconscious, and stealing their narcotics, is relatively complex, and the episode, which Webb directed, combines many elements of *Dragnet's* major themes. Friday is an exemplary policeman; he plans the sting operation that catches the drug addicts and provides the usual amount of narrative control over the story.[29] As usual, Friday calms victims with his example of poise, and, as usual, police procedure is fed into the narration. We see Friday and Smith working on telephones, banks of secretaries processing data, and Friday planning strategy with his superior officer.

When Friday and Smith finally catch the drug addicts, the story shifts, emphasizing the early-1950s film noir style that Webb integrates into many of the episodes. The male suspect fires three times at Friday and Smith while Friday drops to the floor and pulls his gun from its holster. The suspect turns toward a window to escape, and at *that* point, Friday fires his gun. No one mentions this fact later, but Friday has shot the suspect in the back. The suspect's partner (his wife or girlfriend) angrily accuses a shamefaced Friday ("He was just a kid! The whole thing was MY idea! I hope you're proud of yourself now!"). Upon returning to the station, Friday is obviously rattled for the only time in the series; he is distracted and unable to remember the ten-digit case number. When Friday's girlfriend, Ann Baker, enters the office, Smith greets her and, although puzzled at Friday's reaction, offers to fill out the shooting report. The conversation that Friday then has with Baker draws out his character's relationship with the audience and the LAPD. Although Friday is an exemplar of the civic virtue that Parker identified with the LAPD, the second half of this episode places him within the context of average citizens. The relationship between Friday and the audience becomes more complex, emphasizing Friday's position as a regular human being who has to struggle to maintain an LAPD mode of civic excellence.

Baker immediately recognizes the problem; she asks how old the suspect was. Friday responds by telling her that this was "the first time I ever killed a man." She attempts to raise his spirits by making an argument based on professionalism: "You're in a special kind of job"; "the only reason they aren't filling out a report on you or Frank is that you were better at your job than that boy was at his." Friday starts by making contrary arguments and then lapses into a shamefaced silence. He is incapable of rebutting Baker's points, as the Parker framework is assumed within all *Dragnet* scripts; "barbarism within" must be combated for the sake of Western civilization, and the LAPD is the vanguard of the battle. Nevertheless, the sacrifices of the position are clearly drawn on Friday's face; he is positioned within the framework of the larger audience. Providing a model for the city is hard work, and Webb is anxious to show that Joe Friday is not exempt from the price of that work. This episode is a rebuttal to critics' charges that Friday is robotic, or that his actions are beyond the capabilities of average citizens.

Friday's gloom is not relieved, but at the episode's conclusion, Baker convinces him to go to dinner. On the way out of the office, he asks her: "It's kinda dark. Can you find your way?" "Yeah," she responds, "can you?"

The *Dragnet* theme swells at that point and Webb cuts to a picture of Friday's badge. This episode provides a fictional depiction of Parker's worldview: Los Angeles is a dark place, endangered by crime and violence. The only way out is the example of civic excellence that, through popular culture, he provides to the rest of us in the exemplary policeman, Joe Friday. Friday is in fact capable of regret and human feeling, like the ordinary "Joes" in the audience. His cold efficiency is his method of rising to what is required of him, as the rest of us must.

Parker's larger emulatory view did not survive to the end of his tenure as chief and was not passed on whole to the chiefs who followed him. When *Dragnet* returned to network television in 1967, it once again captured the mood of the LAPD. This mood was a new one, however, as we see in the changes made in a new version of the episode described above. In the later episode, Friday goes out for a pack of cigarettes and surprises a petty thief breaking into a vending machine. The thief fires on Friday; he shoots back and fatally wounds the suspect. The entire episode demonstrates how an unashamed (and romantically unattached) Joe Friday almost loses his job because the police forensic team cannot find the bullet that proves the suspect fired first. He provides several long speeches about the thoroughness of LAPD's self-regulation and defends himself against an Internal Affairs investigation. At the episode's end, an investigator finds the bullet and Friday is exonerated of the charge of excessive force. The argument of the show has nothing to do with Friday as a person, and there is no ambiguity about his actions; rather, the episode is an angry reaction to criticism of the LAPD's use of deadly force. *Dragnet* in its run from 1967 to 1970 was a defense of the police force and of a particular ethos; it was not an emulatory challenge.

Parker's loss of faith in emulation and Los Angeles came to a head in 1965, during the uprising in Watts. On August 11, a California Highway Patrol officer pulled over a twenty-one-year-old African American man named Marquette Frye on suspicion of driving under the influence. It was a hot night in Watts, and several people were on their front porches nearby while the CHP officer, Lee Minikus, administered a DUI test and arrested Frye. Frye became angry; the crowd, growing in size, did as well. Thinking that Frye was trying to escape, another CHP officer struck Frye in the face with his baton and tried to push him into the patrol car; at that point, Frye's brother punched Minikus in the kidney, and Frye's mother tore the officer's shirt. Another officer threw a woman into his patrol car for, he charged, spitting at him. When the CHP left, the angry crowd continued to grow, throwing rocks and bottles at police and other white motorists. It was the beginning of an uprising in Watts that, over the course of three nights, spread throughout South-Central Los Angeles and eventually over forty-six miles of the city. For the first time since the Otistown wars, the subject Others of Southern California turned to a form of military-style violence of their own. In Dominick's words, "people were shooting at police officers, hurling Molotov cocktails and sniping at firemen, burning buildings, setting whole blocks on both sides of the street ablaze, breaking windows, looting stores, overturning cars, beating innocent people."[30] They were also responding, through insurrection, to a decades-long strategy of elite control of the public spaces of Los Angeles and a consistent policy of segregating those spaces and of using violence and public policy to colonize the Southland's nonwhite population.

In his first responses to the national media after the Watts insurrection began, Parker referred to himself as "the only police chief that they ever sacked a whole city to get rid of," and told a *Newsweek* reporter that "we had better give the police the support they deserve or the next time this happens, they will move in and sack the whole city." He argued that the majority of the city was opposed to the actions taken in the riots; he also blamed the events of August 11 on the inexperience and poor leadership of the California Highway Patrol.[31] But the predominant notes in Parker's postriot comments are apprehension of new enemies and growing doubt that his exemplary city could be attained.

Parker argued that bad leaders had misled the Los Angeles African American community.[32] The chief had never put much stock in the ability of nonwhites to participate in civic virtue. Even in the early 1950s, Parker argued that proactive policing included acknowledging that certain segments of the population—primarily African Americans and Latinos—were "statistically more likely" to commit crimes. Nevertheless, and despite the fact that his policies suggested as much from the beginning, Parker was careful not to suggest that particular racial or ethnic groups were incapable of being law-abiding; rather, he argued that it was the responsibility of ethnic clergy to provide models for their parishioners away from their "wild tribal" roots and toward whatever civic excellence they were capable of achieving (in a separate portion of the city from white citizens).[33] His most notorious description of the riot ("The riots started when one person threw a rock and then, like monkeys in a zoo, others started throwing rocks")[34] suggests that the rioters were only engaged in violent and subhuman mimicry, but his attempt to defend that statement in the press makes it clear that he had come to believe that a *majority* of American citizens were mimicking vandals, not models of virtue:

> I know better than to cast aspersions on any people in our city. I was referring to the history of riots and particularly the Boston riot where two hours after the police were taken out of Boston someone broke a window and stole a pair of shoes. And then everyone emulated this activity and followed suit and within two hours the city was totally looted, and this was not a Negro riot.[35]

The model of the cities, Parker argued, was barbarism, not civic virtue, and pseudoleaders were winning battles that his LAPD was not.

Parker's 1965 account of his failed attempts to rescue the character of Los Angeles was far more pessimistic and explicitly racist than the most millenarian of his early-1950s historical allegories:

> It's estimated by 1970 that Los Angeles, just to show that I'm interested in more than what the penal code says; that 45% of the metropolitan area of Los Angeles will be Negro, that excludes the San Fernando Valley. Now how are you going to live with that without law enforcement? This is the lesson that we refuse to recognize, that you can't convert every person into a law-abiding citizen. If you want any protection in your home and family in the future, you're going to have to stop this abuse, but you're going to have to get in and support a strong police department. If you don't do that, come 1970 God help you![36]

Parker had conceded a defeat that fifteen years previously he had disallowed; not everyone, not even all whites, can be converted to real citizenship.

In 1950, Parker had concerned himself with behavior; Americans were growing self-indulgent, and they needed to follow a good model back to civic virtue. In 1965, in the aftermath of the Watts uprising and a storm of calls for his resignation, Parker argued that humans are inherently evil. On the television program *Newsmaker,* he stated, "If you want to believe that the human being will respond to kindness with kindness, that he's not an evil thing, you are just living in a fool's paradise."[37] After Watts, the chief abandoned emulatory ambition. If humans were "inherently evil," the best strategy for a police force was to train citizens to preserve the social order they inherited. Parker began drinking more and became less able to conceal the fact. When he died on July 16, 1966, Los Angeles was being "scrutinized through the nation" as a victim of internal dissension and riot. Lessons were being learned that were entirely different from those the chief intended.

The Parker ethos was not completely put to rest with his death, but his hostility toward the citizens of Los Angeles became increasingly central to the politics of Southern California. The LAPD was still trumpeted as an exemplary agency, but the active relationship that Parker had posited between the force and the city was shunted aside. Increasingly, chiefs and departmental spokesmen portrayed the LAPD as a defensive corps trying to hold its own in a hostile environment. Like Otis, Parker had brought the experience of importing colonial mimesis to a conquered population back with him from foreign wars to domestic ones. Now Parker's legacy, like Otis's, was to become the attempt to impose "colonial mimicry"—out of the "desire for a reformed, recognizable Other, as a subject of difference that is almost the same but not quite"—on an ever-widening circle of colonized subjects. If the local residents could not be trusted to act like LAPD officers, they would be instructed to copy models that would *defer* to LAPD officers. If Angelenos would not strive to fulfill Parker's ideal Los Angeles, they would have to copy a model of passivity in order to maintain Parker's ideal police force. Nowhere is this shift more apparent than in *Dragnet,* which, ten years after its first incarnation went off the air, began to be produced once more by Webb and the Office of the Chief.

The new *Dragnet* (titled *Dragnet '67, Dragnet '68,* and so on) does not actually pick up where the old series left off. In 1957, Joe Friday was promoted to lieutenant, but ten years later, Friday is a sergeant. He has a new partner; no mention is made of Frank Smith. Where before the show's LAPD was a group of elite citizens performing difficult tasks, the force in the new show is defensive and victimized. Webb makes this point in one of the first episodes, which originally aired on April 28, 1967. As the audience watches police technicians checking files and processing data, we hear Joe Friday's opening narration: "This is the city. Los Angeles, California. In a city of three million people, thirty-five thousand are known rapists, murderers, and thieves. They outnumber the police force seven to one." The story shifts immediately to a rookie policeman being shot by "pill-popping drifters."

Friday must exert enormous energy to maintain control of the narration in the new *Dragnet*. In the 1950s, Friday could guide the audience with a combination of voice-overs and terse interrogatory grunts; as we saw in the June 17, 1957 episode, Webb could even leave certain story elements ambiguous, drawing audience members into a more empathetic relationship with the characters. By 1967, Webb was no longer this secure. Friday speechifies to an enormous degree, often against representatives of the anti-LAPD counterculture. Three episodes are all dialogue, as Friday argues against drug use with Timothy Leary–like "drug gurus." In the episode that first aired on May 1, 1968, Friday lectures a witness on the psychological causes of compulsive gambling and lectures a compulsive gambler on the need to pray. When a burglary suspect (a "hippie") shows contempt for the court process in the August 12, 1969 episode, Friday provides a three-minute speech on the U.S. Constitution. In the episode for June 26, 1967, Friday tells a drunk driver, "You were hurrying when you ran over that old couple, and now you're hurrying to forget it. Well, mister, I hope it takes you the rest of your life." In two episodes that first aired in 1968, Friday lectures young mothers on their irresponsible methods of raising their children; the women submit to, but do not imitate, his moral position. Rather than demonstrating the path to virtue for ordinary citizens, Friday 1967-70 carefully and angrily excoriates the corruption of the hostile city he is employed to "protect and serve."

Webb attempts in the new *Dragnet* to bring his show up-to-date. In place of the old noir overtones, he edits in psychedelic lighting and music. Friday knows hippie slang and even translates it for his new partner, Bill Gannon (Harry Morgan). But there is no assumed connection with the audience as there was in the 1950s.[38] No one in the episodes produced in the late 1960s adopts Friday's method of analyzing events as characters had in the 1950s; at most, they submit to his arguments. Webb even experimented with two episodes depicting the home lives of the two policemen; both slipped into a domestic situation comedy style, which the show never did in the 1950s, despite occasional scenes of comic relief. The connection between police show and life in Los Angeles was impossible to maintain.

Webb tried to maintain emulation as a feature of the show only in regard to one topic: race. In several episodes, Friday and Gannon have to deal with race relations (arresting a Nazi in the episode for September 15, 1967; showing other policemen how they were behaving in a racist manner), but both of them are extremely stiff; only from their lectures, not from their behavior, could any audience member derive any ideas for action.[39] In the episode first aired on July 15, 1969, however, the idea of emulation in police service is resurrected when Friday uses a black patrolman, Dave Evans, to attract other black men to police service. When Evans considers dropping out of the force, the black civilians abandon their plans. When Evans manages to defuse a potential "race riot," however, and humiliates a black "agitator," the young black men he spoke to earlier join the force, pass their exams, and become patrolmen as well.[40] It is noteworthy that Evans possesses self-doubt as well as dedication to public service; he is one of the few policemen that Webb attempts to humanize in the late-1960s episodes. Even in this episode, however, we can see how empty Parker's emulatory ideal has become. The former chief had wanted to create ideal citizens who would compete with an exemplary police force; in 1969, citizens were not deemed trustworthy enough, and the ambitions of the LAPD became far narrower. The new ideal called for a passive population, a manageable threat. As Friday tells Evans, "Everyone you straighten out now, you might not have to handcuff later."

In trying to exemplify virtue that can run contrary to "hippies" and anti-LAPD feeling, Webb presents his audience with inhuman figures of rectitude. Despite his somewhat robotic nature in the 1950s, Friday could still be presented as comparable to his audience; at no time in the 1960s does Friday unbend as much. In short, the later *Dragnet,* like the policies of the later LAPD, prescribes only the state of submission citizens learn through colonial mimesis. Webb still attempts to replicate reality, copying police cases and procedures with the assistance of the Office of the Chief, and Friday often tells people the proper way to behave, but he is too distant from audience members and even supporting characters to be a model for emulation. If the good victim, witness, or audience member of the show in the 1950s began to speak and frame events as Friday did, the good victim, witness, or audience member in the 1960s submits to the force of Friday's argument and behaves in the manner that Friday prescribes. Rather than emulating an exemplary citizen, who pays a price for his actions but tries to maintain a degree of civic excellence, the ideal audience member of *Dragnet '67–70* would learn to obey the law from the show's model of unrepentant and moralistic deference to authority.

Friday may be remote and virtuous, but the model he proffers is not. In the 1950s, the citizens at home could strive to emulate the citizens on television as they strove to emulate Friday. In the later show, the citizens on television never emulated Friday; they deferred to him. Those characters were the models for the citizens at home; Friday, meanwhile had degenerated from an emulable figure to an allegorical representation of "authority." Audience members would learn these lessons not to become Parker's ideal citizen for the nation, but so they "might not have to be handcuffed later." A new definition of the ideal citizen similarly emerged in LAPD policy: an apolitical figure who would generally remain out of the public realm, but who could imitate models of quiescence when he or she did enter that world. If Angelenos could not emulate stories on TV, Webb suggests, then perhaps they could be trained to behave correctly by the same device.

The only institution whose authority Webb questions in the later series is the courts. The reading of Miranda rights replaces "just the facts" as the mantra of *Dragnet '67–'70,* and although Friday and Gannon are scrupulous about delivering the Miranda speech, Webb's resentment is made clear on a number of occasions.[41] In this, Webb is voicing an obsession of the new L.A. chief of police, Ed Davis. According to Davis, the Miranda ruling was merely one of a number of attacks on police departments by an alliance of left-wing subversive organizations and Washington elites. The brief administrations of Davis, Tom Reddin, and Thad Brown in the late 1960s and early 1970s were noticeably free of emulatory rhetoric; indeed, from Davis's statements we may infer that he felt that the LAPD was isolated from the population at large, and that such isolation was inevitable and, in certain ways, preferable.[42]

When Chief Daryl Gates was still a rookie with the LAPD, he served as Chief Parker's driver, and the two spoke often about police work. Gates would later refer to this part of his career as a "tutorial on how to be chief."[43] Parker saw Gates as a "model policeman" and provided him with innumerable impromptu lectures on police work and ethical responsibilities.[44] For Parker, it seems, this young model policeman provided a perfect opportunity to teach by example, to create a young would-be chief who could continue the good fight. In Gates's words, Parker "didn't have any children, and I think he saw in me an opportunity to mold somebody."[45] What Gates seemed incapable of understanding was that Parker intended to mold an entire city, or that Parker had more than a merely crime-free Los Angeles in mind.

Although Gates saw himself as a disciple of Parker's, his civic vision was far more narrow and hierarchical than that of any Angeleno elite since Otis. In his autobiography, *Chief: My Life in the LAPD,* Gates writes about the aspects of Parker's tenure that he considered most important. The first was the concept of proactive policing, which Gates significantly reinterpreted. Whereas Parker had argued that stopping individuals who seemed like they might commit crimes was part of a policeman's moral duty to forestall the corruption that lay at the root of all crime, Gates saw it as a clever tactical maneuver:

> Due to the small size of the LAPD, Parker thought it would be far more effective to try to stop crime before it happened. . . . Using these pro-active tactics, LAPD would become the most aggressive police department in the country.[46]

Gates maintained the idea that the LAPD had an important job to do that went beyond arresting criminals, but the focus of the job as Parker defined it was lost on him.

The second of Parker's ideas to make a great impact on young Daryl Gates was the idea that the LAPD was an "embattled minority":

> Those speeches had a major impact on me. When Parker explained how the police were a minority, with all the injustices heaped upon a minority, I began to have a sense, finally, of what police officers were all about. . . . 'When violence had occurred, there is the inevitable attempt to blame the police,' Parker said. . . . Wouldn't it be better, Parker suggested, if the public could view the police not as its nemesis, but as its employees? Paid by the people to do what the people wanted done. But didn't care to do themselves.[47]

From Parker's original perspective, however, nothing could be worse than the citizenry's seeing LAPD officers as paid underlings dealing with unpleasant tasks. In his theory of policing, the LAPD was intrinsically connected to the citizens of Los Angeles, and if those citizens did not soon learn to follow in the LAPD's footsteps, the city was doomed to the fate of Babylon and Rome. Nothing could be further from Parker's concept of citizen emulation than Gates's vision of a bitter and victimized LAPD in the dark places of the city, carrying out tasks the citizens would never know about and could never understand. Gates's interpretation of Parker's concept of the embattled minority, however, was of a piece with his speeches after motorist Rodney King was beaten into submission by several LAPD officers in March 1991: clannish minorities or ungrateful taxpayers criticized the police because they did not appreciate that the force made their lives easier by doing the dirty work of the city.[48] The Rampart Division scandals of 2001 arose directly from this vision of policing—LAPD officers who framed, beat, and shot suspected gangsters were doing the "dirty work" of an occupying force in an ungrateful city.

In 1986, in a speech to members of the LAPD assigned to investigating gangs, Gates said that policing Los Angeles is "like having the Marine Corps invade an area that is still having little pockets of resistance."[49] Gates, concerned with tactical questions of how an "embattled minority" could achieve its mission in a city of hostile or uncaring residents, returned to the military model once employed by Otis. Whereas Otis's vision of the military integrated citizens into the soldiery, however, Gates exempted nonpolicemen entirely. There were no self-made men here, no successful journeymen like Mulholland or Chandler. The LAPD was the occupying army, and the citizenry were the occupied residents. Indeed, Gates resented any attempt by the citizenry, in public hearings, or by elected officials to question what his "marine corps" was doing for the citizens' own good. His fights with Los Angeles Mayor Tom Bradley, in particular, were bitter, with Gates threatening that the police would rebel against the city if he were removed from power.[50]

It became apparent from his interviews on *Newsmaker* and *Meet the Press* that Chief Parker saw the Watts uprising as the embodiment of the wrong sort of model being imitated on a wide scale. Watts and its aftermath destroyed Parker's vision of an emulatory relationship between Angelenos and their police force. The Watts uprising, however, was the *foundation* of Gates's views on the LAPD and on the ideal Los Angeles citizen. During the riots, Gates established a command post, encircled himself with patrol cars, and cut off the radio from which Parker was sending his orders. Critical of the riot plan Parker had worked out, Gates began his own attempt to deploy squads of police officers into riot-affected areas. His opinion was that "we're only going to get control through sheer numbers and sheer force," and he argued that the attempts of "community leaders" to "reason" with rioters would be inadequate to the problems at hand. From that point on, as the frustrated battle-scene commander, concerned with sheer force and "turning the people back" and annoyed by the interference of community leaders, from ministers to Parker, who wanted to "reason" with the people, Gates followed a new course in policing.[51]

By the late 1960s, Gates writes, "the streets of America's cities had become a foreign territory. Urban riots signaled one kind of disorder, but we also had civil rights actions, sit-downs, and student uprisings and protests of every kind . . . the police were caught in the middle."[52] No longer public servants, Gates's LAPD had become a group of passive victims, caught in the crossfire of hostile armies in a decaying city. Under the circumstances, the chief and his force were going to take no chances. Thus when two patrolmen confronted Eulia Love on January 3, 1979 (less than a year after Gates became chief), they were prepared for violence. Love had struck an employee of the Southern California Gas Company that afternoon when he attempted to shut off her gas for nonpayment of a bill for twenty-two dollars; the police found her in her front yard with a boning knife and approached her with their guns drawn. According to the officers at the scene, Edward Hopson and Lloyd O'Callaghan, Love was verbally abusive and attempted to throw the knife in their direction; they responded by shooting her eight times, including once after she had hit the ground. In the early Gates years, Dominick reports, other (primarily nonwhite) Angelenos were shot to death by the police for "wielding such items as liquor decanters, wallets, sunglasses, gloves, a hairbrush, a silver bracelet, a typewriter, a belt, a key chain, even a bathrobe."[53] The police force was occupying enemy territory; the chief had been sure of that since 1965. The officers would take no chances with a population that was not merely colonized, but hostile.

It was in this environment that Gates made his first major innovation within the LAPD, creating the Special Weapons and Tactics, or SWAT, team. The officers assigned to SWAT underwent training similar to that the U.S. Army used for Special Forces teams (which John Wayne had made famous in his Vietnam War film, *The Green Berets*). SWAT was supposed to be the LAPD's crack military-style unit, able to attack an enemy target and neutralize it (rescuing hostages, blowing up drug factories, and so on) as efficiently as possible. The men in SWAT improvised their own weaponry and tools, occasionally borrowing from the army (on their first significant "mission," Gates writes, SWAT borrowed a grenade launcher from Camp Pendleton).[54] In Gates's words, "Here in the heart of Los Angeles was a war zone, something out of a World War II movie, where you're taking the city from the enemy, house by house."[55] The Office of War Information had taken pains in the 1940s to integrate sympathetic citizens of enemy nations into World War II films; the exception were the films set in the jungles of the South Pacific, where the Japanese soldiers were represented as too treacherous and alien to be reasoned with.[56] The war that Gates imagined was one of the latter sort, in which the "jungle" environment was too hostile for the pedagogical politics of imitation to be useful.

Several times in the late 1960s and early 1970s, Gates accompanied SWAT on its missions, during which the team employed military tactics and weapons in assaults on enemy "armies" (such as the Black Panthers and the Symbionese Liberation Army) with whom the police battled for the territory of metropolitan Los Angeles. With the introduction of SWAT, Gates embraced the idea of taking his "army" out of the "gutter" and into the spotlight, but not in the way that Parker and Webb had done with *Dragnet:*

> One thing was certain. That night, SWAT became a household word throughout the world. . . . Soon, other law-enforcement agencies began mounting their own SWAT teams. The whole nation had watched the shootout—live, on network TV.[57]

Other law enforcement officials who had watched Gates's shootout on TV might have wanted to emulate SWAT, but the citizens of L.A. could not very well start their own armies.[58] Gates would, on occasion, excoriate the citizens of Los Angeles for being "lazy and apathetic," but what civic education was he attempting to provide with military metaphors and primetime shootouts?

There were few roles available for citizens in Gates's model of policing.

Suspected gang members were considered to be, in the words of First Lady Nancy Reagan when she observed a drug raid, "beyond the point of teaching and rehabilitating."[59] This was nothing new in LAPD policy, as Chief Parker made clear on *Newsmaker* in 1965. Earlier in his tenure, Parker tried to eliminate the Group Guidance Unit of the Probation Department (which attempted to educate and "improve" ghetto youth) under the assumption that such youth were too far gone to follow decent models of behavior. Police department elites, in short, had long considered African Americans, Asian Americans, and Latinos to be colonial subjects at best, incapable of reaching the highest levels of civic virtue.

Gates broke new ground, however, in the militancy and narrowness of his view of legitimate public activity in Los Angeles. His policies were nothing less than the wholesale implementation of colonial mimicry to the population of Southern California. Indeed, Chief Gates's policies make the essentializing and imperial nature of democratic imitative tradition inescapable: democratic order necessitates education, democratic education necessitates models, and models necessitate authority, the augmentation of foundings. The lessons of founding in Los Angeles suggested to Gates nothing so much as the dangers of "civilian" activism. As ordinary citizens could not go on antiterrorist raids, the primary role he proffered them was that of taxpayers who obeyed the rudiments of the law. Although Parker was contemptuous of citizens of Los Angeles who did not meet the task of emulation, his rhetoric never approached the martial fervor of Gates, who charged that members of Los Angeles' middle class who bought drugs were "aiding the enemy" in time of war and should be "taken out and shot."[60] Parker wanted to raise the population to the level of civic virtue; mobsters could be shot, but citizens must either be inspired or given up as corrupt. In Gates's eyes, a war zone such as Los Angeles gave one no time for such distinctions.

The late 1980s gave Gates the opportunity to take the military metaphor to new lengths. In such programs as Operation HAMMER (which rounded up 1,453 "drug suspects" for offenses ranging from drug possession to delinquent parking tickets), Gates took advantage of the Reagan administration's antidrug campaign to upgrade his activities from the street skirmishes of the 1970s. "This is war," he told a *Los Angeles Times* reporter, and as antigang clamor increased in all areas of Los Angeles, the LAPD increased its military tactics, storming suspected "crack houses" with military weaponry (including dumdums— hollow-point bullets outlawed by the Geneva Convention) and quarantining suspect neighborhoods.[61]

By the time of the 1992 uprising following the not-guilty verdicts returned in the trial of the officers who assaulted motorist Rodney King, Gates had updated his analogies, calling Los Angeles "Kuwait all over again" and likening the LAPD to Operation Desert Storm. At this point in his career, however, Gates's military ardor had cooled. Despite the high-level military equipment in his arsenal, the chief kept most LAPD personnel away from the "war zones" until the arrival of the National Guard. His contempt for the citizens of Los Angeles, "enemy" and "civilian" alike, stood between him and the deployment of his police force; Gates already felt too "besieged" by the city to react to the uprising.[62]

Gates's strategy relied on imitation in a number of ways. For the members of Parker's civic elite—the LAPD—he proffered the model of the military (which Otis reserved for the unambitious and "weak-kneed" citizens). He also argued that imitation of other models was vitally important to the LAPD. The undercover division of the Public Disorder Information

Daryl Gates with battering ram, 1985. Courtesy of Herald-Examiner Collection, Los Angeles Public Library.

Division, for example, required police officers to engage in imitating members of the underworld. An officer investigating gangs of drug dealers needed to create a new identity, forgetting all "police mannerisms and assum[ing], as skillfully as any actor, an entirely new role." In such examples of LAPD intelligence work, the force contradicts the imitative ideal that Parker espoused in 1950; rather than serving as an emulatory model, the LAPD mimics criminals. The same was true, Gates argued, when the police engaged in intelligence operations against "subversive"—albeit legal—organizations (when infiltrating "feeder groups, say an SDS campus group," in order to work their way into the inner cell of "dangerous radicals," for example).[63]

Gates was also concerned about bad models that might encourage the sort of negative unconscious influence that HUAC detected in the movies. The technology that Jack Webb had used for good, Gates feared, was being turned against the LAPD and the citizens of Los Angeles by Hollywood. In Gates's view, popular culture in the late 1970s and early 1980s made drug use seem "cool," thereby encouraging teenagers to join the "enemy." Gates was convinced that Hollywood's message about drugs could be used to guide citizens' behavior. He dealt with this problem by meeting with studio executives and producers, providing simplistic models for them to follow. He believed that citizens could be led to one side or the other in the war on drugs. Comedians would make fun of drug users to decide the issue, not provide an example of virtue that viewers could grapple with; viewers, meanwhile, would copy the comics' ridicule of drug use, absorbing the antidrug message through osmosis. In the examples provided by Gates and HUAC, contempt for the emulatory project and for the possibility of an autonomous political tradition results in an inordinate amount of faith in the popular media's ability to control the actions of audience members.

This model of citizen behavior—mimetic, unemulable, submissive, and incapable of autonomous action—and its importance to Gates's LAPD is exemplified by one of his assistant chiefs, Bob Vernon. I have argued that the crime victims in *Dragnet '67–'70* exemplified the model of deference to authority. Assistant Chief Vernon brings that model into the police force itself. In his 1993 memoir, *L.A. Justice: Lessons from the Firestorm*, Vernon attempts to address the underlying moral issues of the Los Angeles uprising of 1992. He begins by citing the example of Chief Parker and devotes half of his memoir to exploring the spiritual problems (such as "materialism") that lie at the root of "social decay."[64] He also argues that what happens in Los Angeles will be followed by the rest of the nation.[65] Vernon does not follow Parker to the point of urging emulatory action, however.

Throughout his analysis of the way to save Los Angeles (and, through L.A., the nation), Vernon stresses the need for parents and civic leaders to provide good models of behavior. Indeed, he provides a comparison between his father and William Parker, and a discussion of the ways in which each man shaped him for the life ahead.[66] The lesson he teaches, however, is one of humble and childlike acceptance. The most important lesson for good models to teach in Los Angeles, Vernon argues, is submission to authority:

> I believe God speaks to me when I get my orders, or direction, from Daryl Gates. I believe I experience the leading of the Lord when the police commission declares policy or the city council enacts an ordinance. . . . I accept the biblical admonition to submit to authority. I believe that principle implies that God will usually lead me through a chain of command.[67]

Vernon holds the models of his father and Parker aloft and attempts to behave in the way in which he thinks they would have, but he would never attempt to surpass them, or even to question them (unless he feels that a biblical commandment is at stake).[68] He mimics the behavior of the good people to whom he humbly submits, but he would no sooner emulate them than he would attempt to emulate the divine level of the "chain of command." I have argued that Angeleno elites like Harrison Gray Otis imposed what Bhabha calls colonial mimicry on populations they seek to dominate. Assistant Chief Vernon adopts those models himself. Small wonder that he, like Gates, constantly uses the example of children when he discusses imitation.[69] He is concerned with the use of models to mold actors through imitation to behave in a particular way vis-à-vis political elites, but nothing could be further from his examples than the adult give-and-take between a citizen and the model of civic virtue that the citizen wants to surpass.

In the emulatory project, William Parker saw the means to create a city that would teach virtue to the rest of the Republic and defeat corruption, communism, subversion, and crime. By 1992, political imitation was still considered important, even dangerous, by the elites of the LAPD. In the LAPD argument that the jurors deciding the case of the officers who beat Rodney King into submission could not dare to trust their eyes, that only a police official could explain to them the necessity of showering an inert figure with baton blows and taser blasts, we see an indication of how passive the LAPD wanted the citizens of Los Angeles to be (a far cry from Parker's dream of the virtue created by competing citizens and policemen). Nonetheless, even Chief Gates had faith in the ability of passive citizens to follow example: responding to public anxiety about police brutality after the airing of the King videotape, LAPD community liaison Tim McBride instructed the members of Neighborhood Watch groups in the ways they should act if they were arrested. To paraphrase 1969's Joe Friday, any citizens who properly imitated McBride might still get handcuffed later, but the process would be safer for them.

In forty years, the LAPD's vision of the ideal citizen of Los Angeles shifted from a vigilant, nonmaterialistic, self-sacrificing member of the white middle class to a suspect who knew how best to act when in the presence of arresting officers. Convinced that his nation was on the verge of barbarism, William Parker proffered an exemplar to the citizens of Los Angeles and demanded that they emulate it. As time passed and Angelenos did not compete with his model, he combined a faith in his exemplar's superior status with a bitterness toward the citizens it was intended to inspire. By the end of the Parker era, the competitive ideal of emulation remained only in a municipal organization whose members believed themselves to be superior to and set apart from their city. Parker's experiment in political imitation had ended as the experiments of Otis, Mayer, and the Warner brothers before him had ended. Gates coupled Otis's military ideal and HUAC's belief in the power of proper authority and media to control and direct citizens. Despite Parker's intentions (that his policies, like Joe Friday's habits, would be copied and eventually emulated by the citizens of Los Angeles), the scripting of public life in Southern California led to demands for civic withdrawal. In more than one hundred years, from 1890 to 1992, Los Angeles produced several attempts to revive a hallowed pedagogical practice, many permutations of imitation as a living pedagogy for citizenship, and they all serve to underscore the profound distinctions at the heart of democratic education. Learning to act, following

exemplary virtue, and competing with it entail the performance of identities—us and them, member and Other, self-made man and anarchist,
and so on—that reinforce and represent coercive and institutionalized power.
Parker Center (where the LAPD is headquartered), the Dorothy Chandler
Pavilion (home for years to the Academy Awards), the new and corporate-
financed L.A. Public Library, and City Hall share the central public area
that was once Bunker Hill, combining education, performance, political
power, and state violence at the heart of Los Angeles, precisely as they
occupy the center of Southern California's democratic culture.

chapter 4

MORE THAN HUMAN
Blade Runner's *Model Citizens*

The relationship between American politics and American art is very nearly
the reverse of that normally proposed. Politics did not root itself in concrete
social interests, driving literature to fairyland. Rather, American political
conflict was both more fragmented and more rhetorically inflated than that in
Europe. If by realism is meant sensitivity to class and to social constraint, then
antebellum American politics was not realist. American literature took on
critical, political functions in the absence of a realist politics, but that absence
decisively influenced the form of the critical literature itself.

—MICHAEL ROGIN

A merican revolutionary Tom Paine held out a radical dream to the
inhabitants of the "new world": "We have it in our power," he
promised, "to begin the world again."[1] The political rhetoric of
the media elites I have examined in the preceding chapters insisted that
they were offering mere fact, a record of "the world as it is"; newspaper,
film, and television were to be used for reportage, not radical transformation. The city on which they reported, however, was a larger-than-life
metropolis, a city refounded, invented, and maintained by Harrison Gray
Otis, the studio moguls, and Chief William Parker. Institutions of popular media mirrored not the "raw data" of Southern California but the
tightly scripted narrative of a virtuous republican hierarchy. Political
authority in the city they reported was attached to a static civil order in

which a small number of heroic, emulatory elites ruled over a depoliticized population that was educated to follow models of support or demonized and futile resistance. If the news narratives seemed grandiose, so was
the subject matter—the media were reporting on a mimetic utopia on the
shores of America's western frontier.

Late-twentieth-century representations of Los Angeles continued, by and
large, to be gothic accounts of a city that is as much a symbol as an urban
center. Some of the more popular representations, however, mapped out
a dystopian city. Director Ridley Scott's 1982 film *Blade Runner* depicts a
Los Angeles in which the urban sprawl, corporate ubiquity, and ethnic
heterogeneity that are characteristic of Southern California have run wild.
Scott's film also constitutes a vivid picture of the central problem in Los
Angeles' civic culture, but that problem is not smog, neon, or multilingual
residents. It is the residuum of political imitation. Scott's concern with the
imitation of the past is built into the structure of his film. A science fiction
movie that takes place in Los Angeles in the year 2019, *Blade Runner* nonetheless incorporates many of the mannerisms of 1940s film. "It suggests,"
in Kaja Silverman's words, "that the farther we travel into the future the
more profoundly we encounter the past."[2] The film's main character, LAPD
Detective Rick Deckard (Harrison Ford), is obviously derived from Warner
Brothers tough-guy films and the Raymond Chandler and Dashiell Ham-
ett novels that inspired them. The film's production design, while futuristic,
is informed by an imitative legacy: the building in which the powerful
Tyrell Corporation is headquartered is a terraced pyramid; Deckard's apart-
ment has a Mayan-influenced interior design. The characters in *Blade
Runner,* however, are not *consciously* competing with the models (classic
Hollywood film, ancient American civilizations) that structure their world.

Blade Runner posits a world of unconscious imitation; it is as if Judy
Garland's Betsy Booth were acting like a citizen of Carvel in her Manhattan home without recognizing her model or its particular virtues. Deckard
is not striving with the model of Hammett's (and Warner Brothers') Sam
Spade or Spade's ethical code; he is merely aping private eye conventions.
The film implies, furthermore, that Deckard is even less autonomous than
HUAC's or Gates' most slavish supporters. The detective is a "blade runner," a policeman who specializes in the killing of androids ("replicants")
who try to "pass" as human. In classic Warner Brothers mode, the detective
is bitterly resigned to his career. One night, after comforting himself with

whiskey and the "evidence" of history contained in sepia photographs, Deckard passes out; he dreams of unicorns. When Gaff (Edward James Olmos), another blade runner, leaves an origami unicorn outside Deckard's apartment, he is suggesting that Deckard's thoughts are programmed and thus available for LAPD surveillance. Deckard too, Gaff suggests, is an artificial human being imprisoned within the narrative of the city's elite.

The replicants are the only characters in the film that are aware of their predicament and are attempting to resolve it. They are supposed to be "more human than human," designed to emulate their designers by, in Silverman's words, "living out more fully and more consciously than their makers the basic conditions of subjectivity."[3] The renegade replicants that Deckard has been assigned to destroy were sold into slavery in outer space but have returned to Earth to confront their makers. Replicants are designed to die after four years, and they have returned to the Tyrell Corporation, where they were produced, to force Tyrell (Joseph Turkel) to make sense of their lives.

Indeed, it is Tyrell's place in Los Angeles 2019 to make sense of *everyone's* lives. He is *Blade Runner*'s Otis and its Mayer. Programming the replicants with some of his own physical and mental attributes (the childhood memories of the replicant Rachael [Sean Young], for example, are either Tyrell's memories or the memories of his niece), he literally uses his life to craft the identity of a portion of the Los Angeles population. Tyrell is the leading citizen whose sense of history constructs the civic life of Los Angeles, even if the other citizens, like Deckard, do not know it.

"More human than human": Roy Batty (Rutger Hauer) dies in *Blade Runner* (1982).

Through Tyrell's relationship with his city, *Blade Runner* exemplifies the legacy of political imitation in Los Angeles. Tyrell's life sets the terms for the lives of his replicants, but his vision of civic life also affects the human beings who still exist in Los Angeles. The collapse of the moral legitimacy of Gates's Los Angeles Police Department—demonstrated most vividly in the circumstances leading up the trials of O.J. Simpson and of the officers accused of beating Rodney King[4]—arises from the model of virtue established by William Parker. Harrison Gray Otis's story, meanwhile, has constrained the political careers of recent mayors Richard Riordan (Republican) and James K. Hahn (Democrat) through the construction of the valorized models of public life. Indeed, since Otis, the self-made man, an increasingly apolitical, individualist fantasy has haunted the politics of Southern California.[5] The mimetic vision of Los Angeles even constrained the career of L.A.'s most successful modern mayor, the pluralist coalition builder Tom Bradley.

The success of the Bradley coalition was, in part, a reaction to the excesses and exclusions of Los Angeles' mimetic politics. The elites I have discussed in this volume have not had a monopoly on Los Angeles' political life, and their models have been challenged. These elites have attempted to defend their exempla by defining their opposition within the framework of the ideal civic worlds they crafted. Harrison Gray Otis's vision of a city of self-made men was defined against a demonized picture of the "slavery" of organized labor. The unions battled against Otis's vision and his cohort, and almost, in 1911, succeeded in electing a Socialist mayor who would have dismantled the open-shop foundation of the publisher's ideal city.

Organized labor also waged a powerful war against the studios. The political organization of the 1940s was built on foundations laid in the 1930s, when the group of conservatives who would eventually create the Motion Picture Alliance for the Preservation of American Ideals joined with the studio moguls in fighting the new independent unions of screenwriters, actors, and technical personnel. For Mayer, the attempt to unionize was a refutation of the small-town family he strove to create at MGM. When Mayer's daughter refused to divorce her husband after he threw a fund-raiser for Adlai Stevenson, Mayer disinherited her. He was no more forgiving of studio "children" who disobeyed him. He begged Lester Cole, a veteran writer at MGM, to abandon the Hollywood Ten and support

HUAC; he even offered Cole his own production company. When the writer refused, Mayer threw him off the lot. The MGM chief was a supporter of the blacklist; it was an organized way for him to "disinherit" the employees who, he felt, had spurned his fatherly support. In addition, Mayer and the Warner brothers used their films to depict the members of the American left as dupes of the Communist Party or even as spies in the service of a foreign power.

Race was another outside category that the elites I have discussed here attempted to define within the limits of their civic narratives. Michael Rogin has demonstrated how Jewish immigrant entertainers in vaudeville, and later in Hollywood, used blackface as a tool for their own assimilation.[6] As Otis contrasted his ideal form of citizenship to a demonic representation of labor, the major studios and the LAPD contrasted their models with caricatures of racial and ethnic minorities. One such caricature portrayed minorities as overly pliable and incapable of distinguishing between good and bad models. Parker warned that African Americans were following bad leaders who led them to undermine social order and attack the virtuous models he proffered. The LAPD and the Los Angeles news media have similarly characterized the Latino community as unthinkingly imitative and vulnerable to bad models.[7] Nonetheless, Parker and others argued, racial minorities could be good citizens if elites consistently provided them with appropriate models. As Otis learned in the Philippines, even "bumptious natives" can be educated as democratic subjects in the proper colonial context. Civic elites would innovate and emulate; nonwhites, workers, and the "weak-kneed," meanwhile, could embrace colonial models, learning to be like real citizens, but "not quite."[8]

According to Parker, the *Los Angeles Times,* and other newspapers, however, African Americans and Latinos often followed bad models, lacking the character or will to pursue civic virtue. Chiefs Parker and Davis argued that racial minorities were "cannon fodder" for criminal organizations, Communists, and anarchists. The Watts uprising of 1965, Parker argued, was the result of African Americans following bad models like "monkeys in a zoo."[9] Racial minorities were thus presented with two alternative stereotypes within mainstream media during much of the history of Los Angeles' imitative project: the Othered status of Bhabha's colonial mimicry and the blindly imitative and thus irredeemable enemy of LAPD rhetoric.

The citizens caricatured by Otis, Parker, and others opposed the stark division between ideal and inferior citizens, between exemplary and evil models. The Chandler family and its associates constituted a small and relatively impermeable civic elite; Parker and the conservative Jewish film moguls succeeded in creating independent power bases from the Chandler circle, but these civic elites were not inclusive either. African Americans, Latinos, and liberal Jews and WASPs were effectively locked out of Los Angeles' political world. The unwillingness of the elites to attempt to incorporate these groups resulted in a significant and powerful alternative to the Angeleno model of imitative politics.

The initial opposition of the civic elites discussed in this book significantly strengthened the political alliance among African Americans and liberal Jews and WASPs that became known as the Bradley coalition.[10] Tom Bradley was elected mayor of Los Angeles in 1973, promising to create effective citizen oversight of the Police Department, to increase the participation of ethnic minorities in city politics, and to provide more money for impoverished East and South-Central Los Angeles. Bradley achieved these goals for years without increasing local taxes and while supporting the local business community's progrowth policies. Successfully wooing large amounts of federal funding while engaging in the boosterism that has been central to Los Angeles politics since the 1890s, Bradley widened the old economic elites' narrow political world by providing support for them and other citizens. As Raphael Sonenshein describes it, "The coalition became a sort of hybrid: a progressive biracial alliance dedicated to police accountability, affirmative action, environmental planning and antipoverty programs, joined to a moderate elite alliance devoted to growth, downtown redevelopment, and the creation of a 'world-class' city."[11] Bradley was helped in this endeavor by the globalizing economy and the mellowing of the Chandler family, now in its fourth generation at the center of Los Angeles' economic and political elite. Otis Chandler, publisher of the *Los Angeles Times* in the 1970s and 1980s, was more concerned with maintaining L.A.'s international economic importance and the reputation of his paper for unbiased journalism than he was with local politics or exemplary virtue.

If the Chandler family was prepared to adapt its vision of the exemplary city, however, the Los Angeles Police Department was not. The truncated self-made-man ethos of the city's economic elite was able to allow for the success of the Bradley coalition; the mayor had found a way to increase the permeability of the city's leadership without doing damage to the city's oldest model of ideal citizenship. Since the 1965 Watts uprising, however, the LAPD's racist perspective on Southern California had become integral to its definition of civic virtue. The Bradley coalition, in Sonenshein's words, was "the department's worst nightmare come true," a political alliance composed of "racial minorities and liberal reformers . . . the groups against which the LAPD had historically aimed its political efforts."[12] Bradley placed more independent politicians on the Police Commission and successfully lobbied for 1992's Proposition F, which limited the terms of LAPD chiefs and removed their civil service protection. In short, he was largely able to dismantle William Parker's blueprint of LAPD autonomy.[13]

The Bradley coalition is an example of a successful elite alternative to the tradition of political imitation in Los Angeles. Tom Bradley proffered no models of ideal politics and did not use himself as an exemplar for other citizens. Indeed, his customary style of governance was inconspicuous and remote, prompting Sonenshein to characterize Bradley's style as "hidden hand leadership":

> Until recent years, this covert style worked very well in a city where politics had low salience. Bradley's pattern has been to work behind the scenes though a network of people, allowing an issue to take shape and exerting his influence indirectly. . . . Key staff people became his link to evolving issues, and somewhat mysteriously let the mayor's wishes be known.[14]

Not concerned with creating a new model of politics for Los Angeles, Bradley succeeded in adapting one of the city's oldest models.

When the Reagan administration curtailed the federal funds that had been a central facet of the Bradley coalition's success, the mayor's support for progrowth business interests remained in place, but his ability to provide for East and South-Central Los Angeles declined. Although Bradley was a significant force for reform in Southern California, his historical role is comparable to Harry Chandler's. Bradley curtailed the most violent excesses of political imitation, but he did not use his public position to provide a different model of political life. Eschewing political imitation does not resolve its problems. The defensive and contemptuous philosophy of Chief Gates, arising from the degeneration of Parker's exempla, contributed to the events of 1991 and 1992—the beating of Rodney King, the acquittal of his attackers, and the consequent uprising—and the damage they did; adopting the Chandlers' economic model of politics did not help Bradley to escape the consequences of Otis's imperialist model of civic life. Bradley's administration did help to increase citizen participation in the policy-making process in Los Angeles and successfully incorporated more racial minorities into city commissions.[15] But Bradley did not exhort the population to enter the political world; he did not describe what that world might or should look like. Providing no contrary model of politics, Bradley still had to govern a city whose politics were framed by Otis's self-made-man zealotry and the reaction to Hollywood's and Parker's attempts at emulatory inspiration. Walking away from the imitative project is not sufficient to resolve the burdensome legacy of that project.

Where Sonenshein and other pluralist authors have seen the Bradley coalition as an interest-based success story, social critic Mike Davis has seen a continuation of Angeleno economic elitism. Davis's *City of Quartz* is perhaps as popular a vision of Southern California dystopia as Gates's or Scott's. Davis provides a convincing picture of the history of Los Angeles, illustrating the Southland's combination of violence, salesmanship, and economic stratification without reifying the power of the hierarchies I have discussed. Davis understands the power of utopian vision in Southern California, and he also describes—in sometimes overwhelming detail —the dystopias that have been constructed from those dreams. His critique of Otis and the Chandler family is well drawn, and he provides a wealth of evidence for the closed nature of the armed camp created and maintained by Parker, Gates, and even current mayor James Hahn.[16]

In short, Davis understands both the power of elite narratives in Los Angeles and their fictional basis. His diagnosis of Los Angeles, however, is structured by some familiar stories. Davis's reportage at times functions as a camera obscura: he turns mimetic hierarchies on their heads, but he does not escape from them. In Davis's Los Angeles, imperial power is not an American phenomenon directed outward; rather, it is imposed on Americans by an Asian empire. Contrary to the accounts of Sonenshein and other pluralist supporters of the Bradley coalition, Davis argues that the successful L.A. economy of the 1980s and 1990s was part of the city's "colonial subservience" to the sort of cunning enemy faced by OWI platoons in the South Pacific.[17] The "inscrutable" Japanese economy, Davis warns, has created wealth in Los Angeles for its own purposes, and Hollywood, too, has fallen prey to "*zaibatsu*" economists, despite the threat of subjugation and "*kamikaze*" economic collapse.[18] Davis, like Otis, Parker, Mayer, and the HUAC chairmen, occupies a gothic and conspiratorial Los Angeles; his L.A. is a fallen utopia, victim to the power of racially Othered imperial enemies.

Davis does not engage in this rhetoric to provide more reasons for an Otis-style colonial mimesis; indeed, his intent is to strip bare a labyrinth of power, to uncover imperial hierarchies and "industrial slavery." He maps out Los Angeles—in some cases literally—providing a blueprint that seems intended to be liberating and politicizing. In short, his account is structured by the L.A. mimetic style, a realist portrayal of a larger-than-life inverse utopia, but he is intending to renew an adversarial and open-ended politics for Southern California. Scott's *Blade Runner,* in contrast, provides the viewer with a reactionary dystopian vision. Los Angeles 2019 is the victim of racial and linguistic diversity, a city that has lost its connection to its Anglo-American refounding moment and thus to any cohesive community. Scott's narrative has thus been employed by some Southern California elites who seek to reinforce the hierarchies of Otis's city. Indeed, the director's vision of "LA 2019" helps to structure the identity of Tom Bradley's dream of "LA 2000": in the mid-1980s, the mayor commissioned a panel to create "a strategic plan for Los Angeles." The result, presented in a report titled *LA 2000: A City for the Future,* threatens Angelenos with the specter of Scott's dystopia. As Davis describes it:

> The report's epilogue (by historian Kevin Starr) reminds readers that the last "coherent" Los Angeles . . . found "community on a civic level" because it "had a dominant establishment and a dominant population." The report clearly implies that because of the decline of the Anglo *herrenvolk*—i.e. the absence of a dominant culture group in an increasingly poly-ethnic, poly-centered metropolis—a "dominant establishment" is more essential than ever. While explicitly warning of the "*Blade Runner* scenario"—"the fusion of individual cultures into a demotic polyglottism ominous with unresolved hostilities"—the report opts for the utopia of the "Crossroads City": "an extraordinary city of cities, a congregation of livable communities."[19]

In short, dystopian visions and pluralist interest-group politics combine to threaten the city with the anarchic, un-American nightmare metropolis that will result if the Southland cannot maintain the narratives that bind it together. Others will come: they will be taught to be mimetic supportive citizens (or residents)—similar to Angeleno elites, but not quite the same, copies of innovative originals—or they will become an unformed, barbaric, and demonized enemy.

There are two versions of *Blade Runner* currently on the market: the one released by Warner Brothers and the Alan Ladd Company in 1982 and the version originally edited by Scott, which was not released until 1992.[20] The two versions have different endings, but neither succeeds in surmounting the confined imaginary world of Los Angeles 2019. In the "director's cut" version, Deckard and Rachael are going to flee the city, but before they leave the detective's apartment building, Deckard finds Gaff's origami unicorn. The distinction between Deckard and the android has been destabilized; he may well be carrying Tyrell away with him in his thoughts.

In the Warner Brothers cut of the film, we see the couple escape to an idyllic wilderness while Deckard's voice-over informs us that Rachael has been designed without a specific four-year death date. The forest, however, gives the lie to the film's cheery resolution: the detective and his lover have not resolved the burdens of Los Angeles' imitative project, they have merely escaped to an apolitical wilderness. They have no community, no other people, no memories or experiences to replace those that have been implanted by Tyrell.[21]

The only memories in the film that Tyrell is unlikely to have bothered creating are those of the dying replicant Roy Batty (Rutger Hauer), who, after his creation, was sold into slavery: "I've seen things you people wouldn't believe. Attack ships on fire off the Shoulder of Orion. . . . I've watched Sea Bees glitter in the dark near the Tannhauser Gate. . . . All those moments will be lost in time, like tears in rain." At one extreme, Los Angeles 2019 has the burdensome legacy of its elite's ideal interpretation of the city and its citizens; at the other, the fragile and fragmentary memories of the outsider whose history mattered only insofar as he could serve as a contrast to that ideal.

I have lingered so long over the story of *Blade Runner* because it demonstrates the ubiquity of the imitative project and how hard it is to escape.

The Los Angeles exempla of political life reflect and reinforce the modes and models of political imitation that have repeatedly been invoked as central to the founding excellence of the American Republic; the American founders themselves, meanwhile, looked to mimetic and emulatory projects of antiquity. The emulation that fired Romans of the early republic to strive with each other's example was, according to Livy and Plutarch, central to the establishment of a Roman political tradition and to the preservation of Rome in moments of crisis. It was a practice at the core of an Arendtian reading of political authority, augmenting the work of the Roman founding through a mimetic preservation or an emulatory contest. Similarly, in the American Republic, Adams, Washington, and others argued that emulation is intrinsic to human nature and hoped to use their examples and the models with which they competed to create an active and autonomous republic. Nevertheless, by 1838, Abraham Lincoln argued, those models were losing their power and the preservation of the Republic required not competitive striving but a sober and rational dedication to sacralized American law.

The emulatory project in America did not end with George Washington. It did, however, become more difficult. Washington successfully followed the model of Cincinnatus by living the tradition of the heroic citizen-farmer and emulated that model by founding a new republic. Innovating by taking seriously and competing with the models of historical exempla, individuals can create states of great virtue and achieve glory. The most popular model in American history represents an attempt to pursue this course. The model of the self-made man, however, does not necessitate emulation. Imitators of the self-made man could still achieve economic and political virtue without joining the elite circles of the successful emulators. But Harrison Gray Otis intended to create a city of self-made men, an exemplar for the nation, and could not allow for such "weak-kneed" lack of ambition. Otis successfully emulated the self-made man and helped to craft a city he saw as his masterpiece, a metropolis devoted to the propagation of an economically driven form of virtue through the imperial methods of democratic education he had learned in the Spanish-American War. The restricted political world that the *Los Angeles Times* publisher created, the stratified economic realm that was the sole arena of interest for his descendants, illustrates that one of the most popular American models of virtue was antithetical to an active political culture. The necessity of passive obedience on the part of a majority of citizens, the mimetic colonization of Los Angeles' citizens that Otis began, and his hostility to any independent participation in civic life resulted in a city that served as an exemplar of antipolitical occupation.

Harrison Gray Otis pioneered the elite bifurcation of Angelenos into worthy emulators and deferential supporters who learned their place in the city through, in Bhabha's terms, colonial mimicry. Otis demanded the achievement of the impossible task for those who would be active American citizens: to strive to imitate the model that imitates no one. For the rest of Los Angeles, including the majority of the entrepreneurial middle class, the publisher developed a model derived from the military: the dutifully quiescent model of the loyal foot soldier. And central to this project was the power of the new mass media, of newspapers and (soon) Hollywood to provide a perfect replica of the model political community. Educating citizens for democratic action and locating them within a larger membership required the mimetic assurance provided by Webb, like many before him, when he promised his national audiences that this, indeed, is the city.

Aesthetics were an irresistible target for the practitioners of political imitation in Los Angeles. The men who thought they had isolated the exempla that would create new heights of civic virtue throughout the country could not refuse the enormous audiences available through newspapers, movies, and television. In fictional characters, Louis B. Mayer and Harry Warner could create individuals who would personify the characteristics that made up the ideal American citizen. Otis learned important lessons in colonial mimicry during his service in the colonial enterprise of the Spanish-American War; Hollywood took those lessons back to the world stage, offering up models of ideal "Americanism" to the world for its imitative purposes. As Woodrow Wilson had learned in World War I, mass media can mobilize audiences for global warfare. But Hollywood's alliance with the Roosevelt administration to spur citizens to emulate war heroes resulted in a political backlash. According to HUAC, the media were not a way to urge autonomous citizens to strive for virtue but rather a means of mind control. The committee members and the repentant studio chiefs countered the wartime exempla, therefore, with a carefully scripted and controlled refutation of the flurry of independent political activism that occurred in Southern California during the war.

Left-wing and radical politicization was thus attacked and abandoned by Angeleno elites, but mimetic mobilization was not. Chief William Parker pledged in 1950 to use his police force in an attempt to lead Los Angeles and the nation to virtue. Machiavelli hoped to rescue Florence from corruption with models of classical *virtù;* Parker hoped that the example of his police force, for which he proselytized and which was personified in the fictional Joe Friday, would be sufficient to pull Los Angeles back from the brink of barbarism. The virtuous competition between citizens and policemen, the chief hoped, would create a city that could serve as an exemplar for the nation and the world. The model that Parker and his successors offered the public after Los Angeles failed to take up the chief's emulatory challenge, however, does not resemble Florentine emulation of the ancient Romans so much as the Roman occupation of ancient Tuscany. Chief Gates argued that the LAPD's primary task was the imposition of order on an ungrateful occupied city. The model he proffered, therefore, was designed to teach the proper methods of passive deference to authority. His authority was challenged—successfully, in the long run—by the Bradley coalition, but it was designed to augment a mimetic strategy that reaches back to the refounding of Los Angeles and reaches forward to affect the politics of the twenty-first century.

Having ascertained that imitation is unstable and dangerous to political life, that the moments of emulatory virtue are outweighed by the potential for abuse, I cannot say that political actors of the present should eschew "imitating excellent men [or women] in the past" or "holding [oneself] up as a model" in order to "challenge others to imitate."[22] The experience of citizenship as others have lived it, or as they have argued it should be, contains knowledge of our shared civic tradition. Removing ourselves from the opportunity to follow the example of others deprives us of the opportunity to learn political action from history. The models of others, in any case, are not so easily escaped. Parker's exemplar of 1950 helped to create the beating of Rodney King, the crimes of the Rampart Division, and the LAPD's withdrawal from the city it was supposed to "protect and serve." Otis's dreams of a city of self-made men, meanwhile, created the elite coterie at the heart of Los Angeles politics for most of the twentieth century.

The exempla of Los Angeles history structure the political life of Southern California. Politics in Los Angeles must confront the legacies of Otis,

Mayer, the Warner brothers, Parker, and Gates without ceding to them the position of sole civic models for an American metropolis. And, indeed, the Angeleno elites I have discussed in this book wanted Los Angeles to serve as an exemplar that could renew the virtue of the United States. From the self-made man to the products of Hollywood, the tradition of political imitation in Los Angeles has influenced citizens throughout the American Republic. American Los Angeles has roots in Manifest Destiny and the apprenticeship of its refounding elites in the colonial moment of the Spanish-American War, and it is perhaps unsurprising to find mimesis used against the consecutive Others of Southern California history. But the story of Los Angeles also casts light on the significance of this colonial mimesis at the heart of democratic political education. In the pages of the *Los Angeles Times,* in *Andy Hardy Gets Spring Fever,* in the press releases of the Los Angeles Police Department, we see evidence of the democratic authorization of a domestic colonial hierarchy and the influence of the past on the policies offered in the present. *This* is the city, these actors have assured us, and these roles constitute *the* available options for a democratic citizenry. Mimesis provides a democratic rationale for the elimination of autonomous politics, and its narratives are central facets of Angeleno authority; it is not enough to reject them. The resolution of the many crises in the political life of Los Angeles and the reinvigoration of a *virtuoso* political life lie in the continued attempt to understand, challenge, and even enact the unstable, dangerous, promising, and problematic tradition of political imitation.

NOTES

INTRODUCTION

1. Arendt, *On Revolution,* 201.

2. Machiavelli, *Discourses,* bk. III, preface, 419.

3. Machiavelli also recommends the imitation of founding models of virtue and other examples of *virtù* in *The Prince* and *The Art of War.* In chapter 6 of the former, for example, he writes that "since men almost always walk in the paths beaten by others and carry on their affairs by imitating—even though it is not possible to keep wholly in the paths of others or to attain the ability of those you imitate—a prudent man will always choose to take paths beaten by great men and to imitate those who have been especially admirable, in order that if his ability does not reach theirs, at least it may offer some suggestion of it." Ibid., 24.

4. The Latin root of the word is *vir* (man), and it connotes some of the same attributes as *virile* and *virtuoso.* Ibid., 11; *Cassel's Latin/English Dictionary.* In *Fortune Is a Woman,* Pitkin brilliantly illustrates the effects of a defensive and undermined masculinity at the heart of the many paradoxes in Machiavelli's work. Bonnie Honig employs the distinction between virtue and *virtù* to move beyond Machiavelli, providing both a devastating reading of the liberal/communitarian split in political theory and a compelling account of the attempts to fix political action that I examine through the paradox of republican mimesis. See Honig, *Political Theory.*

5. Machiavelli, *Discourses,* I.4, 202–4.

6. In the preface to book I of the *Discourses,* Machiavelli presents us with a splendid example of this paradox. Within one paragraph, he promises to "enter a path not yet trodden by anyone" and to remind his readers to imitate "the most worthy activities" of "ancient kingdoms and republics" (190).

7. Cicero, *On the Commonwealth,* II.42, 193.

8. Ibid., II.40–42, 191–93.

9. Ibid.

10. Later in the same text, Cicero clarifies his definition of civic duty: "Our own generation, after inheriting the commonwealth as if it were a painting, of unique excellence but fading with age, has not only failed to restore its original hues, but has not even troubled to preserve its outline and the last vestiges of its features." Ibid., V.1, 243.

11. *Oxford English Dictionary; Cassel's Latin/English Dictionary.* The ancient Greek word that most closely approximates "emulation," *zeloi,* also connotes imitation, rivalry, and jealousy.

12. In *The History of Rome from its Foundation,* for example, Livy states that the heroism of Gaius Mucius against the Etruscans was so great that it inspired "the women of Rome to emulate him," and their heroism in turn was an example of virtue for the young Republic (I.13, 120). Similarly, Livy demonstrates how Rome survived a two-front attack by the Volscians and the Sabines through the striving of each Roman legion to emulate the other: "In Rome there was rejoicing, but the effect of the news was even more notable on the troops under Horatius' command, as it fired them to emulation" (III.69, 252).

13. Quoted in ibid., III.21, 208.

14. Plutarch's *Lives of Famous Greeks and Romans* also provided moral and political exempla to readers in the early years of the empire. Indeed, by composing the *Lives* in parallel fashion, coupling the history of notable Greeks and Romans with similar virtues, Plutarch introduces a competition of civic excellence into the very structure of his work. Like Nicocreon and Pasicrates, who appear in *The Life of Alexander,* the subjects of Plutarch's work "show great emulation to outvie each other," thereby providing models for readers who may emulate them in turn. It is for this reason that Plutarch directs his attention only toward events that illustrate the character of his subjects; he designed the *Lives* to be a moral education by example through which readers could participate in the book's emulatory competition. See Plutarch, *Lives,* esp. *Life of Alexander,* 139. Nicocreon and Pasicrates appear on p. 162 of the same edition.

15. See Arendt, *On Revolution,* 187, 197; Fliegelman, *Declaring Independence;* Wills, *Cincinnatus;* Pocock, *The Machiavellian Moment,* 508; Wood, *Creation of the American Republic,* 46–90. Wood notes: "At one time or another almost every Whig patriot took or was given the name of an ancient republican hero, and classical references and allusions run through much of the colonists' writings, both public and private. It was a rare newspaper essayist . . . who did not employ a classical signature" (49).

16. Paine, *Common Sense,* 51.

17. Wood, *Creation of the American Republic,* 50, 106; Wills, *Cincinnatus.*

18. Arendt, *On Revolution,* 196, 198.

19. Wood, *Radicalism of the American Revolution,* pt. III.

20. Fliegelman provides a striking example of this shift: in the 1820s, Federalists charged Jefferson with plagiarism in his draft of the Declaration of Independence. When Jefferson defended his authorship of the document as "an expression of the American mind" whose principles and language were drawn from "the harmonizing

sentiments of the day, whether expressed in conversation, in letters, printed essays, or in the elementary books of public right, as Aristotle, Cicero, Locke, Sidney, etc." (Jefferson to Henry Lee, May 8, 1825), he was adhering to an older concept of authorship. As the public insisted on a definition of authorship as the creation of something altogether new and free of any imitation, overt pedagogical imitation in the civic realm became increasingly suspect. *Declaring Independence,* 165.

21. David Ramsaye to Archbishop John Tillotson, quoted in Wood, *Radicalism of the American Revolution,* 235.

22. Fliegelman, *Declaring Independence,* 105.

23. Lincoln, speech to the Springfield Young Men's Lyceum, in *Political Thought of Abraham Lincoln,* 20.

24. Ibid., 19.

25. Ibid., 18.

26. Ibid., 21.

27. Ibid., 19.

28. Wills, *Lincoln at Gettysburg.*

29. Honig, *Political Theory,* 77.

30. Mimesis is "the name of the active personal identification by which the audience sympathizes with the performance." Havelock, *Preface to Plato,* 26. In Havelock's words, "The poetic performance if it were to mobilize all [the] psychic resources of memorization had itself to be a continual reenactment of the tribal folkways, laws and procedures, and the listener had to become engaged in this reenactment to the point of total emotional involvement" (159). See also Jaeger, *Paideia,* chaps. 3, 5, and 8; see esp. p. 310.

31. Wilson, "The Ideals of America," 732–34. See also Rogin, "The King's Two Bodies," in *Ronald Reagan,* 91, 314.

32. Machiavelli's injunction to emulate the ancients provides an interesting insight into this process. Machiavelli frequently proffers the Romans as models of *virtuoso* politics. Pitkin points out, however, that in imitating the Romans Machiavelli is identifying with the invaders who extinguished the *virtú* of his native Tuscany. The successful emulation of the ancients by sixteenth-century Florentines would build the glory of that city from the model of the conquerors that wiped out Tuscany's native civilization. See Pitkin, *Fortune Is a Woman,* 272–73. In *Discourses,* Machiavelli adds that if the imitation of the Romans is too high a target to pursue, ancient examples can still be used to create *virtú* and glory in contemporary Italy: "Yet if the imitation of the Romans seems difficult, that of the ancient Tuscans ought not to appear so, especially to the present Tuscans because, if the former could not . . . set up an empire like that of Rome, they were able to gain in Italy the power that their manner of proceeding yielded to them. This was for a long time secure with the utmost glory of authority and arms, and with the highest reputation in manners and religion" (III.4, 339). To say that Tuscany's founding excellence, the virtues of its pre-Roman history, is a fair second-best target for decadent contemporaries reflects the power that successful conquest can have over even imagined native exempla for the would-be patriot.

33. Sir Edward Cust, "Reflections on West African Affairs . . . addressed to the Colonial Office," Hatchard, London, 1839, quoted in Bhabha, *Location of Culture,* 85.

34. Bhabha, *Location of Culture,* 85–92.

35. "Prepared Statement of Harry M. Warner, President of Warner Brothers Pictures, Incorporated, to the Subcommittee on Interstate Commerce, United States Senate; Regarding Moving Picture Propaganda," September 25, 1941.

36. William Parker, speech to the Holy Name Society, Los Angeles, January 1953.

37. Gates, *Chief,* 110, 286–87, 383–84.

38. Ibid., 47.

39. Honig, *Political Theory,* 24.

1. A CITY OF SELF-MADE MEN

1. Bhabha, *Location of Culture,* 56.

2. See Sanchez, *Telling Identities;* Pitt, *Decline of the Californios;* Mariano Guadalupe Vallejo, *Documentos para la historia de la Alta California,* 1874, Bancroft Library Collection, University of California, Berkeley.

3. See Jackson, *Ramona;* Jackson, *Echoes in the City of the Angels,* excerpted in Ulin, *Writing Los Angeles.*

4. Rogin, *Fathers and Children,* 258.

5. Wood, *Radicalism of the American Revolution,* 235; Fliegelman, *Declaring Independence,* 105.

6. See Wyllie, *The Self-Made Man,* 9–10; Register of Debates in Congress, Washington, DC, 7, 1, 277.

7. Michael Rogin demonstrates the connection between emulation's ubiquity and the economic and political ambitions of American citizens: "Liberal society, as Adam Smith and John Adams had described it, progresses by emulation. Always unsatisfied with their present condition, men copied the successes of others and sought to improve themselves. They internalized personal ambition and the desire for the good opinion of others." *Fathers and Children,* 207.

8. See Wyllie, *The Self-Made Man,* chap. 3; Lear, *No Place of Grace;* Trachtenberg, *Incorporation of America.*

9. "But of all the virtues that adorned the life of this great man, there is none more worthy of our imitation than his admirable INDUSTRY. . . . This was the life, this the example set by Washington . . . YOUNG READER! go thy way, think of Washington, and HOPE. Though humble thy birth, low thy fortune, and few thy friends, still think of Washington, and HOPE. Like him, honour thy God, and delight in glorious toil." Weems, *Life of Washington,* 203–15. Wood briefly discusses this chapter, "Washington's Character Continued: His Industry," in *Radicalism of the American Revolution,* 283.

10. Quoted in Wyllie, *The Self-Made Man,* 129–32. Franklin's autobiography was widely read, as were such books as Hubbard's *A Message to Garcia,* Conwell's *Acres of*

Diamonds, Matthews's *Getting on in the World,* Maher's *On the Road to Riches,* and Thayer's own *The Poor Boy and the Merchant Prince.*

11. Wyllie cites the following in *The Self-Made Man,* chap. 5: Frank Ferguson, *The Young Man* (1840); Daniel Wise, *The Young Man's Counsellor* (1854); P. T. Barnum, *Struggles and Triumphs* (1869); Thomas Mellon, *Thomas Mellon and His Times* (1885); and John D. Rockefeller, *Random Reminiscences of Men and Events* (1909).

12. Miller, "Otis and His *Times,*" 5, 10, 11, 14–28; Gottlieb and Wolt, *Thinking Big,* 17–18; Otis, "Milestones," 1.

13. Otis, "Milestones," 2–3; Miller, "Otis and His *Times,*" 7.

14. Otis, "Milestones," 1–3; Miller, "Otis and His *Times,*" 10–11.

15. Abraham Lincoln, letter to Mrs. Lydia Bixby, November 21, 1864.

16. Abraham Lincoln, speech on the Kansas-Nebraska Act, 1854, in *Political Thought of Abraham Lincoln,* 76.

17. Otis, "Milestones," 11; Miller, "Otis and His *Times,*" 14–18; Gottlieb and Wolt, *Thinking Big,* 18–19.

18. Gottlieb and Wolt, *Thinking Big,* 19. See also Miller, "Otis and His *Times,*" 29–41.

19. It was in Santa Barbara, for example, that he carried on the fight to provide votes for Rutherford B. Hayes with editorial statements such as the following: "Let tomorrow prove that the dead soldiers of the Republic were not sent to their bloody graves for naught. . . . Young man, you who will tomorrow cast your first vote, beware of the shameless old harlot misnamed Democracy. . . . Spurn the hardened hag . . . and flee to the arms of Hayes and Wheeler." *Santa Barbara Daily Press,* November 6, 1876. For Otis, the language of moral purity, economic autonomy, and loyalty to the Republic and the Republican Party were indivisible.

20. Gottlieb and Wolt, *Thinking Big,* 20–21, 26–27; Miller, "Otis and His *Times,*" 88–107.

21. Miller, "Otis and His *Times,*" 119; Gottlieb and Wolt, *Thinking Big,* 46.

22. Miller, "Otis and His *Times,*" 111–14; McWilliams, *Southern California,* chap. 9; Vaniman, "Southern California Land Boom."

23. See Miller, "Otis and His *Times,*" 270; "A Letter from Harrison Gray Otis," 1914, private correspondence, Bancroft Collection, University of California, Berkeley; *Los Angeles Times,* July 20, 1909; *Los Angeles Times,* February 23, 1908; *Los Angeles Times,* September 14, 1907.

24. Machiavelli, *Discourses,* II.2, 332–33.

25. Miller, "Otis and His *Times,*" 119, 156–65; Gottlieb and Wolt, *Thinking Big,* 56–64.

26. Gottlieb and Wolt, *Thinking Big,* 56. For an extensive discussion of the San Pedro fight, see also Miller, "Otis and His *Times,*" 119, 156–65.

27. For example: "Are the citizens of Los Angeles slaves and curs that they should permit themselves to be whipped into line by Colis P. Huntington? Is this a community of free and independent American citizens, or are we the vassals of a bandit, creatures

open to bribery, slaves to a plutocratic master, who has neither bowels of compassion, common decency, nor an organ in his putrid carcass so great as his gall?" Quoted in Miller, "Otis and His *Times*."

28. Miller, "Otis and His *Times*," 168–73; Gottlieb and Wolt, *Thinking Big*, 21–24.

29. In one letter, Otis stated, "These ignorant, misguided, and bumptious natives . . . wantonly assailed the authority of the Republic." Private correspondence, quoted in Gottlieb and Wolt, *Thinking Big*, 22. In a *Times* editorial, he asserted: "The average Filipino is not a bad fellow, nor wholly without merit or intelligence. He certainly has rights to be respected, and I believe that, properly managed, good can be got out of him, for himself and for the country." Quoted in Gottlieb and Wolt, *Thinking Big*, 22.

30. Bhabha *Location of Culture*, 86.

31. McWilliams, *Southern California*, 272–78; Gottlieb and Wolt, *Thinking Big*, 32–33; Miller, "Otis and His *Times*," 128–39.

32. Otis, *Story of the Distinct Victory*, n.p.

33. See McWilliams, *Southern California*, chap. 14, esp. pp. 273–84.

34. Shortly after Morrow of the *Express* and Holder of the *Tribune* settled with the LATU, Otis wrote Markham of the *Herald:* "Had it not been for the unspeakable cowardice and the inexcusable treachery of our confreres of the *Tribune* and the *Express* we might today be complete masters of the situation with the strikers minus a foothold in our town. As it is, the *Times* and the *Herald* stand together and will fight it out. Principle and manhood require it." See Miller, "Otis and His *Times*," 135; Gottlieb and Wolt, *Thinking Big*, 36. The *Herald*, however, settled shortly thereafter.

35. Gottlieb and Wolt, *Thinking Big*, 37–40. Gottlieb and Wolt quote a *Times* editorial to illustrate Otis's stance on labor disputes: "The lines must be drawn. Let men who love their country and mean to support it take their stand and take it quick."

36. Miller, "Otis and His *Times*," chap. 4; Gottlieb and Wolt, *Thinking Big*, 40–42; Starr, *Inventing the Dream*, 72–73.

37. Good overviews of M&M history appear in Miller, "Otis and His *Times*," 192–200; Davis, *City of Quartz*, 28, 31, 113–14, 120; McWilliams, *Southern California*, 178–80. However, superior accounts are provided by Gottlieb and Wolt, *Thinking Big*, 45–47; and Kahrl, *Water and Power*, 170–79.

38. McWilliams, *Southern California*, 278; Starr, *Inventing the Dream*, 74, 86, 125.

39. Gottlieb and Wolt, *Thinking Big*, 45.

40. Kahrl, *Water and Power*, 174; Miller, "Otis and His *Times*," 217–24. A September 1903 law required police permits for street meetings, and the LAPD denied permits to any organizations that the M&M opposed. After the LAPD created Earl Hynes's Red Squad, it was able to provide an independent line of attack; the squad, employing spies and thugs, inflicted enormous damage on radical and liberal political movements in Southern California.

41. Quoted in Kahrl, *Water and Power*, 171.

42. Quoted in Gottlieb and Wolt, *Thinking Big*, 46.

43. Gottlieb and Wolt provide an anecdote that illustrates the influential position of the M&M: "Businessmen were so fearful of the M&M/*Times* power that, on one

occasion, a company—the Senthouse Packing Company—got a court injunction to force the unions to remove its name from a union 'fair' list." *Thinking Big*, 46. See also McWilliams, *Southern California*, 277–83; Miller, "Otis and His *Times*," 372–75; Kahrl, *Water and Power*, 170–79.

44. See Miller, "Otis and His *Times*," 270.

45. See, in particular, Rogin, "Political Repression in the United States," in *Ronald Reagan*, 44–80; Slotkin, *Fatal Environment*, esp. pts. 3, 6, 7.

46. *Los Angeles Times*, January 22, 1911.

47. See Gottlieb and Wolt, *Thinking Big*, 80–83; Kahrl, *Water and Power*, 173; Mowry, *California Progressives*, 49–55.

48. Miller, "Otis and His *Times*," 363–69.

49. Specifically, the council banned "picketing, carrying or displaying banners, signs, or transparencies, or speaking in public streets in a loud or unusual tone for certain purposes." Quoted in Gottlieb and Wolt, *Thinking Big*, 83.

50. Miller, "Otis and His *Times*," 389–91; Kahrl, *Water and Power*, 170–75.

51. In an editorial the day after the explosion, Otis addressed the enemy in terms far more vituperative that any he had used in the Civil or Spanish-American Wars: "O you anarchic scum . . . you cowardly murderers, you leeches upon honest labor, you midnight assassins, you whose hands are dripping with the innocent blood of your victims." *Times*, October 4, 1910.

52. The IBSIW was the sole metals-related union that had not knuckled under to the powerful U.S. Steel/National Erectors' Association combination, and for five years the two forces had been engaged in a bloody conflict. More than one hundred construction sites had been bombed, and the NEA had blamed the McNamaras for those bombings. Burns's testimony came from an IBSIW employee, Ortie McManigal, whom he had threatened to charge with murder in connection with the *Times* bombing. Gottlieb and Wolt, *Thinking Big*, 89–96; Kahrl, *Water and Power*, 174–79.

53. Miller, "Otis and His *Times*," 413–16; Gottlieb and Wolt, *Thinking Big*, 89–96; Starr, *Inventing the Dream*, 174–79.

54. Burns, *The Masked War*, 11, 135, 319, cited in Miller, "Otis and His *Times*," 425–33.

55. Bhabha, *Location of Culture*, 91.

56. See Kahrl, *Water and Power*: "It is very doubtful, however, that the Socialists could have achieved . . . much success in so resolutely conservative a community as Los Angeles without . . . the artful use Harriman made of [Water Commissioner William] Mulholland's aqueduct as a symbol for all that was wrong and corrupt in the existing order. Harriman once again brought out all the charges raised in the bond elections of 1905 and 1907 concerning the financing of the project, the adequacy of its design, and the quality of the water it would deliver. More important, he charged that the project was unnecessary, that the flows of the Los Angeles River were sufficient to serve the city's needs . . . and that the aqueduct had been promoted in the first place for no other reason than to benefit the San Fernando land syndicate" (173). See also Miller, "Otis and His *Times*," 441–48; Davis, *Rivers in the Desert*, 75.

57. Miller, "Otis and His *Times*," 456–63; Kahrl, *Water and Power*, 175, 189–200; Davis, *City of Quartz*, 112–14.

58. Miller, "Otis and His *Times*," 464–77; McWilliams, *Southern California*, 180–81; Gottlieb and Wolt, *Thinking Big*, 96–105.

59. *Los Angeles Times*, December 6, 1911.

60. *Los Angeles Times*, September 14, 1907; *Los Angeles Times*, February 23, 1908; *Los Angeles Times*, July 20, 1908.

61. Gottlieb and Wolt, *Thinking Big*, 121–26; Kahrl, *Water and Power*, 186–88; Miller, "Otis and His *Times*," 140–50; Davis, *Rivers in the Desert*, 102.

62. Gottlieb and Wolt, *Thinking Big*, pt. 2; Kahrl, *Water and Power*, chap. 5; McWilliams, *Southern California*, 133, 136, 157; Davis, *City of Quartz*, 114–20; Davis, *Rivers in the Desert*, 101–4.

63. Gottlieb and Wolt, *Thinking Big*, pt. 2, esp. pp. 124–26; Starr, *Material Dreams*, 102–3.

64. Kahrl, *Water and Power*, 20. See also Starr, *Material Dreams*, 50–51; Davis, *Rivers in the Desert*, 107–12.

65. Kahrl, *Water and Power*, 21.

66. Quoted in ibid.; Davis, *Rivers in the Desert*, 109. Margaret Davis's *Rivers in the Desert* is proof of the endurance of Mulholland's legend as the embodiment of the self-made man. Davis's description of the engineer as a "common working man" who had "come West to seek his fortune," who also had a "paternalistic responsibility for Los Angeles" and served as a "mythic figure" and model of hard work for the local citizens, draws out the nineteenth-century aspects of the self-made-man role, the figure who combines the "hard work and pluck" aspects of the story, which are still popular, with the antiquated idea of a figure of social, political, and pedagogical centrality (3–8, 29–32, 112). According to Davis: "William Mulholland was the realization of the American ethic of industry and self-education, an original American persona who became an integral part of the mythology surrounding the creation of modern Los Angeles. Rugged, fearless, and determined, he was a self-realized man of the West, a genius of the people. Like many of them, he had been a mere immigrant starting out with nothing more than a strong back and a willingness to work" (107–8).

67. Eventually, Mulholland would also serve as a cautionary tale: unwilling to delegate authority or to trust others to handle matters of which he considered himself master, the water commissioner failed to find structural flaws in the St. Francis Dam. More than three hundred lives were lost when the dam collapsed on March 12, 1928, and Mulholland's reputation never recovered. See McWilliams, *Southern California*, 194–96; and Kahrl, *Water and Power*, 311–19.

68. Gottlieb and Wolt, *Thinking Big*, 127–34; Kahrl, *Water and Power*, 103; Starr, *Material Dreams*, 48–56; McWilliams, *Southern California*, 187–88.

69. In fact, rainfall levels in Southern California were normal, and there seems to have been little danger of a drought. Kahrl, *Water and Power*, 85–103, 182, 266; Gottlieb and Wolt, *Thinking Big*, 131–34; Starr, *Material Dreams*, 56–61.

70. "The cable that has held the San Fernando Valley vassal for ten centuries to the arid demon is about to be severed by the magic scimitar of modern engineering skill,"

boasted Otis in 1905. As the aqueduct progressed closer to the city, readers became quite familiar with the "genius of the people" that wielded that scimitar. Kahrl, *Water and Power*, 79–94; Davis, *Rivers in the Desert*, 5–68.

71. *Los Angeles Times*, August 10, 1905.

72. McWilliams, *Southern California*, 188–90; Gottlieb and Wolt, *Thinking Big*, 134–40; Kahrl, *Water and Power*, 89–103. As I noted in the introduction to this volume, the story is also the basic outline for director Roman Polanski's 1974 film *Chinatown*.

73. *Los Angeles Times*, November 5, 1913.

74. "A Statement by Mr. and Mrs. Chandler," Los Angeles, 1914, Bancroft Collection, University of California, Berkeley, 13.

75. Gottlieb and Wolt, *Thinking Big*, 123–24.

76. Pitkin, *Fortune Is a Woman*, 273.

2. HOLLYWOOD IN THE 1940S

1. The most influential of the studio moguls were Harry Cohn of Columbia Studios; William Fox of Fox Studios; Carl Laemmle of Universal; Louis B. Mayer of Metro-Goldwyn-Mayer; Harry, Al, Jack, and (briefly) Sam Warner of Warner Brothers; and Adolph Zukor of Paramount.

2. Gabler, *Empire of Their Own*, 82–83; Selznick, *A Private View*, 4; Higham, *Merchant of Dreams*, 5–11.

3. Selznick, *A Private View*, 27; See also Gabler, *Empire of Their Own*, 85–89; Higham, *Merchant of Dreams*, 14–22.

4. Higham, *Merchant of Dreams*, 66–67; Gabler, *Empire of Their Own*, 110.

5. Mayer signed, for example, the popular child star Mary Miles Minter; Hollywood's leading woman director, Lois Weber; and, in a major coup, Lillian Gish. Higham, *Merchant of Dreams*, 40–44, 91–92; Gabler, *Empire of Their Own*, 108–9. As Kevin Brownlow notes in *The Parade's Gone By*, "Metro-Goldwyn-Mayer achieved, within a few months of its inception, a prestige envied by every other company" (490).

6. Memo from Mayer to Weber, quoted in Gabler, *Empire of Their Own*, 109.

7. Quoted in Higham, *Merchant of Dreams*, 70.

8. In the words of Danny Selznick, Mayer's grandson, Mayer saw MGM's films as tools for "shaping the taste of the country. . . . the one part of life in Communist Russia he would have admired if he had stayed behind was the way in which art is forced to shape society. . . . He wanted values to be instilled in the country and knew how influential films could be and very much wanted to capitalize on it." Quoted in Gabler, *Empire of Their Own*, 216.

9. Director Billy Wilder, for example, later recalled seeing Mayer shaking young actor Mickey Rooney by the lapels, screaming at him, "You're Andy Hardy! You're the United States! You're the Stars and Stripes! Behave yourself!" Quoted in Gabler, *Empire of Their Own*, 216. See also Ray, *The Avante Garde*, 157.

10. Higham, *Merchant of Dreams*, 74, 78, 123–24, 209, 205; Gabler, *Empire of Their Own*, 111–12.

11. Selznick, *A Private View*, 64; Gabler, *Empire of Their Own*, 88.

12. Higham, *Merchant of Dreams,* 50, 77.

13. Brownlow, *The Parade's Gone By,* 484; Gabler, *Empire of Their Own,* 80. Edith in her youth hoped to be an entertainer on the stage, and Mayer paid for her to take a series of acting, singing, and dancing lessons. When she announced her intention to perform in New York, however, Mayer forbade it, declaring, "You're the best goddamned actress of them all. And you need it for living." The important and exemplary work of MGM, it seemed, required that the Mayers live public lives; the stage was superfluous and would require a potentially damaging mixing of roles. See Gabler, *Empire of Their Own,* 106–7; Higham, *Merchant of Dreams,* 92–93.

14. Higham, *Merchant of Dreams,* pp. 59, 68, 219, 258. Mayer also joined Chandler's longtime business partner Harry Haldeman in investing in the larcenous Julian Petroleum Corporation. A significant percentage of Los Angeles' financial elites participated in the Julian "stock pool" scheme, issuing and purchasing more than five million shares of fake stock to drive up the worth of their shares in the company. The collapse of Julian ruined hundreds of small local investors. See Higham, *Merchant of Dreams,* 104, 116, 125; Tygiel, *Great Los Angeles Swindle,* esp. 183–84, 202.

15. Mayer spoke at the Republican national convention in 1928, promising to "deliver the motion picture industry" to the Hoover campaign; he thereby infuriated other moguls as well as the president of Loew's, Nicholas Schenck, who was a supporter of the Democratic Party. Higham, *Merchant of Dreams,* 132 (see also 34, 70, 78–80, 164); Gabler, *Empire of Their Own,* 115–16.

16. Gabler, *Empire of Their Own,* 220–36; Brownlow, *The Parade's Gone By,* 483–90. MGM director Clarence Brown claimed that "nobody ever touched Thalberg" for film production genius, and pioneer screenwriter Anita Loos wrote: "Thalberg was the greatest man in pictures. We used to have a preview every week at MGM. Fifty-two previews a year. If a picture proved a failure in the studio, he knew how to fix it. By the time it hit the screen outside, it was great. He had a completely fresh viewpoint on everything. . . . I was with him for eight years, and when he died, I said 'Hollywood is finished. I'm going to get out.' And I did." Both Brown and Loos are quoted in Brownlow, *The Parade's Gone By,* 488. Indeed, Thomas Schatz argues that Thalberg all but invented the studio system by creating a central production process at MGM that the rest of the industry was forced to copy. Schatz, *Genius of the System,* 29–47, 98–124, 159–73.

17. *American Weekly,* summer 1955, quoted in Higham, *Merchant of Dreams,* 423.

18. Higham, *Merchant of Dreams,* 291; Ray, *The Avante Garde,* 2–3.

19. The seventh film, *Andy Hardy Gets Spring Fever,* is credited to W. S. Van Dyke II, director of some of MGM's more famous movies in the early 1930s (such as *Manhattan Melodrama* and *The Thin Man*), but Mayer replaced Van Dyke with Seitz only two weeks into filming for attempting to change the Hardy formula.

20. Celebrities such as Mickey Rooney, whom Mayer excoriated for failing to imitate Andy Hardy's virtues in real life.

21. Some of which (*Trader Horn* and the first of the Johnny Weissmuller Tarzan films, for example) were directed by nominal *Spring Fever* director Van Dyke.

22. Higham, *Merchant of Dreams,* 70.

23. Ray, *The Avante Garde,* 148.

24. Ibid., 160.

25. Glassman, "Afterword," 266.

26. Gabler, *Empire of Their Own,* 216.

27. See Jefferson's letter to W. S. Smith, November 13, 1787: "A lively and lasting sense of filial duty is more effectually impressed on the mind of a son or daughter by *King Lear,* than by all the dry volumes of ethics and divinity that ever were written." Quoted in Arendt, *On Revolution,* 323.

28. Brownlow, *The Parade's Gone By,* 490.

29. Harry Warner remembered "his father telling him, 'Son, you're going to have to fight with the weapon you have at your command so that the children and their children may have a right to live and have a Faith, no matter what that Faith may be, in our great country, America.'" Gabler, *Empire of Their Own,* 123.

30. "Warner Brothers," *Fortune,* December 1937. See also Gabler, *Empire of Their Own,* 120–22; Behlmer, *Inside Warner Brothers,* 55, 64. Warner and studio executive assistant Walter MacEwen also argued that social-problem films and gangster films had a cathartic quality that would reduce the urge to commit criminal acts in impressionable youth. See Behlmer, *Inside Warner Brothers,* 129–30. Gabler argues in *An Empire of Their Own* that this statement was disingenuous, but if so the artificiality of this pose had no effect on Warner's public persona. He and others at the studio repeated such statements and did try to present models publicly for both the imitation and the avoidance of their audiences.

31. Rosten, *Hollywood,* quoted in Koppes and Black, *Hollywood Goes to War,* 1.

32. Vice president in charge of production Jack Warner was a very partisan Democrat and a booster of Roosevelt. Whereas MGM's films were announced by the roar of Leo the Lion, Warner Brothers movies began, after 1932, with an image of FDR's "NRA Eagle." The Warners were the first to offer their services to the Roosevelt administration when World War II began, and they swiftly worked to adapt the studio's most popular genres to the exigencies of wartime citizenship. The Warners even dubbed the popular 1933 musical *42nd Street* a "New Deal in Entertainment."

33. Gabler, *Empire of Their Own,* 197–98; Behlmer, *Inside Warner Brothers,* 188. Jack Warner loved *The Maltese Falcon* film ("a hell of a good picture") and tried to convince Dashiell Hammett to write a sequel. Plans were also made to insert the character of Sam Spade into other Warner Brothers films. See Behlmer, *Inside Warner Brothers,* 157–59.

34. Indeed, his primary response to his secretary regarding the death is to ask her to "have 'Spade and Archer' taken off the door and 'Samuel Spade' put on."

35. Roosevelt, *FDR's Fireside Chats,* 150–51.

36. Memo from Jack and Harry Warner to President Roosevelt, May 20,1940, quoted in Gabler, *Empire of Their Own,* 343. Indeed, even before Roosevelt's speech, Warner Brothers had released mainstream Hollywood's first anti-Nazi film, *Confessions of a Nazi Spy* (1939), against the protests of the industry's self-censoring Production

Code Administration and the German embassy. See Koppes and Black, *Hollywood Goes to War,* 28–29.

37. Ceplair and Englund, *Inquisition in Hollywood,* 18–19.

38. Ibid., 89–90.

39. Ibid., 88–93. See also Mitchell, *Campaign of the Century.*

40. Quoted in Ceplair and Englund, *Inquisition in Hollywood,* 84. See also Hamilton, *Writers in Hollywood,* 107–10; Gabler, *Empire of Their Own,* 328–29.

41. Hamilton, *Writers in Hollywood,* 108.

42. The Front was composed of Democratic New Dealers, Socialists, and members of, among other organizations, the Hollywood Anti-Nazi League, the Motion Picture Democratic Committee, the Communist Party of the United States of America, and the Hollywood Independent Citizens Committee of the Arts, Sciences and Professions.

43. *History of the American Film Industry,* Hampton, 349; Gabler, *Empire of Their Own,* 342; Ceplair and Englund, *Inquisition in Hollywood,* 109–10. After Germany officially banned U.S. films, MGM promptly released *The Mortal Storm* (1940). Appropriately, Mayer's first anti-Nazi film demonstrated the poisonous effects of Nazism on the nuclear family, the foundation of virtue in the Andy Hardy series and many other MGM films. Jack Warner later claimed to have urged his fellow studio chiefs to oppose Germany openly in 1939 and 1940; see Friedrich, *City of Nets,* 49–50. Warner Brothers had one intimate reason for breaking off its relationship with Germany; Joe Kaufmann, the studio's representative in Berlin, was murdered by Nazis. See Gabler, *Empire of Their Own,* 342; Ceplair and Englund, *Inquisition in Hollywood,* 110; Friedrich, *City of Nets,* 48. The Warner brothers also advocated opposition to the Nazis because of Hitler's policies toward the Jews. Mayer, on the other hand, avoided any mention of anti-Semitism in his comments on Germany and the war.

44. Gabler, *Empire of Their Own,* 344–45; Ceplair and Englund, *Inquisition in Hollywood,* 159.

45. Senator Gerald Nye, speech reprinted in *Vital Speeches of the Day,* September 15, 1941, 720–23; Gabler, *Empire of Their Own,* 345; Koppes and Black, *Hollywood Goes to War,* 39–41; Ceplair and Englund, *Inquisition in Hollywood,* 159–61.

46. "Prepared Statement of Harry M. Warner, President of Warner Brothers Pictures, Incorporated, to the Subcommittee of the Committee on Interstate Commerce, United States Senate; Regarding Moving Picture Propaganda," September 25, 1941; Behlmer, *Inside Warner Brothers,* 188–91; Koppes and Black, *Hollywood Goes to War,* 17–18, 40–45; Gabler, *Empire of Their Own,* 345–47.

47. Koppes and Black, *Hollywood Goes to War,* 49–50.

48. Ibid., 59.

49. Ibid., 63, 77, 112.

50. Ibid., 64.

51. The OWI manual included seven questions that were supposed to guide filmmakers: "1. Will this picture help win the war? 2. What war information does it seek to clarify, dramatize or interpret? 3. If it is an 'escape' picture, will it harm the war effort by creating a false picture of America, her allies or the world we live in? 4. Does

it merely use the war as the basis for a profitable picture, contributing nothing of real significance to the war effort and possibly lessening the effect of other pictures of more importance? 5. Does it contribute something new to our understanding of the world conflict and the various forces involved, or has the subject been adequately covered? 6. When the picture reaches its maximum circulation on the screen, will it reflect conditions as they are and fill a need current at that time, or will it be out-dated? And 7. Does the picture tell the truth or will the young people of today have reason to say they were misled by propaganda?" Quoted in ibid., 66–67. The "young people" of which the memo speaks are, or course, supposed to be led by propaganda, but not *misled;* note the way that mimesis—the proper understanding film should provide of "the world we live in"—is seen as a central part of Hollywood's role in helping the U.S. win its war.

52. *Variety,* December 10, 1942.

53. Koppes and Black, *Hollywood Goes to War,* 108–9. The studios and OWI were harmoniously collaborating by the end of the war, when Davis used his power of film export to help the studios reestablish their European markets as the Allied soldiers marched in. See Koppes and Black, 140–41.

54. Harry Warner's testimony before the War Propaganda Subcommittee, September 25, 1941.

55. In a scene that Mayer originally wanted Wyler to tame, Mrs. Miniver tries to reason with and even care for the pilot, who seems to be the same age as her son. Her motherly response is typical of any 1930s MGM domestic heroine, but is inappropriate to the new situation. After rummaging through the kitchen for food, the pilot begins to brag about his part in the destruction of Belgian towns: "Others come . . . like me . . . thousands! And we will do the same thing here!" Faced with an implacable and swarming enemy, audiences need to reassess the small-town homilies of MGM's civic ideals.

56. The dead were not infrequently used as models in World War II. One bond advertisement, for example, featured a photo of a dead soldier with the caption, "I died today. What did you do?" Polan, *Power and Paranoia,* 45.

57. Hamilton, *Writers in Hollywood,* 219.

58. Warner Brothers used the funeral oration format in other films as well. Humphrey Bogart delivers one in an OWI favorite, *Action in the North Atlantic* (1943): "Any one of us could be lyin' here and somebody read the book over us and be tossed in the sea. That ain't what's important. A lot more people are gonna die before this is over, and it's up to the ones who come through to make sure that they didn't die for nothing."

59. Polan, *Power and Paranoia,* 155–57. Polan, in fact, attributes Rick's liminal position to the "hesitation of the Hollywood machine at this moment." Rick's position certainly demonstrates a transitional moment, a story that combines the film world of the Depression with the wartime heroism of the 1940s. The Hollywood studios did hesitate at the war's beginning—some more than others—but their ability to adapt their old narratives rapidly to the war effort was striking.

60. Ceplair and Englund, *Inquisition in Hollywood*, 121.

61. Testimony given before the House of Representatives Committee on Un-American Activities, 80th Congress, October 1947, quoted in ibid., 181.

62. Ceplair and Englund, *Inquisition in Hollywood*, 121.

63. HR 198, 73rd Congress, March 20, 1934; U.S. House of Representatives, *The House Committee on Un-American Activities*.

64. HUAC's anti-Communism and anti-Semitism were at times indistinguishable. At one hearing, the committee chair attempted to establish the subversive nature of many Hollywood liberals merely by listing their names: "One of their names is June Havoc. We found out from the motion-picture almanac that her real name is June Hovick. Another one was Danny Kaye, and we found out that his real name was David Daniel Kaminsky. . . . There is one who calls himself Edward Robinson. His real name is Emmanuel Goldenberg. There is another one here who calls himself Melvyn Douglas, whose real name is Melvyn Hesselberg." Quoted in Ceplair and Englund, *Inquisition in Hollywood*, 289; Gabler, *Empire of Their Own*, 371–72.

65. Gabler, *Empire of Their Own*, 351–63; Ceplair and Englund, *Inquisition in Hollywood*, 109–115.

66. Koppes and Black, *Hollywood Goes to War*, 66–69, 144; Ceplair and Englund, *Inquisition in Hollywood*, 97. The Motion Picture Alliance was founded by anti-Communist director Sam Wood, and the membership included Walt Disney; actors Barbara Stanwyck, John Wayne, Clark Gable, Irene Dunne, and Ginger Rogers; director John Ford; and International Association of Technical and Stage Employees president Roy Brewer.

67. Friedrich, *City of Nets*, 166–68; Ceplair and Englund, *Inquisition in Hollywood*, 97.

68. Neal Gabler recounts the meeting between Harry Warner's son-in-law, producer Milton Sperling, and FBI agents in the mogul's office: "As Sperling recalled it, 'Harry said, "They got it on you." I said, "What do they got on me?"' Harry threw a sheet of paper across the desk. On it was a list of the various liberal organizations Sperling had joined. Beneath these was his service record: he had volunteered for the U.S. Marine Corps and had been discharged as a captain. And beneath that was a single sentence: 'Sperling is a premature anti-Fascist.'" Even service in the armed forces, apparently, was potential evidence of subversive tendencies. Gabler, *Empire of Their Own*, 366.

69. The Ten were Alvah Bessie, Herbert Biberman, Lester Cole, Edward Dmytryk, Ring Lardner Jr., John Howard Lawson, Albert Maltz, Samuel Ornitz, Adrian Scott, and Dalton Trumbo.

70. Ceplair and Englund, *Inquisition in Hollywood*, chap. 8; Gabler, *Empire of Their Own*, 368–70.

71. Ceplair and Englund, *Inquisition in Hollywood*, 289; Gabler, *Empire of Their Own*, 371.

72. Ceplair and Englund, *Inquisition in Hollywood*, 291; Gabler, *Empire of Their Own*, 370–74; Hamilton, *Writers in Hollywood*, 292–93.

73. Gabler, *Empire of Their Own*, 374–79.

74. Quoted in Ceplair and Englund, *Inquisition in Hollywood*, 384.

75. Ibid., 384, 373–74.

76. Quoted in Gabler, *Empire of Their Own*, 356–57.

77. Thomas was eventually imprisoned for defrauding the U.S. government by collecting salaries for nonexistent employees; he eventually served time in Danbury Prison with Hollywood Ten member Lester Cole. Ceplair and Englund, *Inquisition in Hollywood*, 356.

78. Mayer was hostile toward and skeptical of the new MGM leadership. He opined to a reporter: "I know what the audience wants. Andy Hardy. Sentimentality! What's wrong with it? Love! Good old-fashioned romance." Quoted in Gabler, *Empire of Their Own*, 412.

79. Roddick, *New Deal in Entertainment*, 87.

3. THE BADGE

1. Machiavelli, *Discourses*, bk. III, preface, 421.

2. Webb, *The Badge*, 246–53; Dominick, *To Protect and Serve*, pt. 2.

3. In the latter case, a group of Chicano teenagers were arrested and convicted en masse of the murder of another Latino youth; the police provided no hard evidence, and the presiding judge refused to allow the teens to wear suits to court, or even to shower beforehand, for fear that doing so would camouflage their essential nature as gangsters. See Escobar, *Race, Police*, 272–83; McWilliams, *Southern California*, 314–29. The zoot suit riots were a three-night pogrom in East Los Angeles, in which police officers and servicemen pulled young nonwhite men from streetcars, movie theaters, and restaurants and pummeled them because of alleged attacks by Mexican Americans on U.S. soldiers. The attacks occurred during World War II, in the midst of the Roosevelt administration's "Good Neighbor Policy" toward Latin America, and the president eventually demanded an imposition of martial law to stop the attacks. See McWilliams, *Southern California*, 319–20; Escobar, *Race, Police*, chap. 12.

4. Parker saw himself as part of a historical tradition of American virtue, bringing civilization to a lawless frontier, and he was skilled at imparting this self-image in the media. Jack Webb's treatment of Parker's background is typical: "His grandfather, William Henry Parker, had been one of the great frontier peace officers when there was no middle ground between right and wrong. After the gunslingers had been quieted, he had gone on to Washington as a Congressman; so the boy knew that, though the fight may be dangerous, courage and honesty win out in the end.

"From old-timers he heard stories of outlaw and Sioux, showdown and massacre; and he knew the Valley of the Little Big Horn, Hay Stack Butte, Sundance Creek, Buffalo Gap, and the Belle Fourche. Though the frontiersmen were now old and garrulous, he caught their tough, impatient spirit, and it was to mark him for life." Webb, *The Badge*, 245. Parker could not quite portray himself as an exemplar in the tradition of his grandfather and namesake, however, the "Wild West" was an unsettled portion of a young nation, whereas Parker argued that in his own time, the United States had already grown old and corrupt.

The biographical data on Parker provided here are derived from Webb, *The Badge;* Dominick, *To Protect and Serve;* Gates, *Chief;* Parker, *Parker on Police.*

5. By the 1980s, police salaries would take up almost 18 percent of the municipal budget; see Sonenshein, *Politics in Black and White,* 160.

6. Indeed, Parker argued that public relations and public education were central parts of police work, and he set forth his civic philosophy whenever the opportunity arose. "During the first few years in office, by former LAPD deputy chief Harold Sullivan's account, Bill Parker would make over a thousand speeches. He'd go to breakfasts, lunches, and dinners and speak before crucial groups such as the Chamber of Commerce, the Downtown Business Men's Association, and the Merchants and Manufacturers' Association. He'd even travel out to the city's distant reaches in the Valley and the South Bay, leaving no stone unturned in his efforts to promote the LAPD, expand its power, and transform its image." Dominick, *To Protect and Serve,* 103.

7. William Parker, "Religion and Morality,"speech delivered to the Holy Name Society, Los Angeles, January 1953.

8. Machiavelli, *Discourses,* III.1, 421.

9. William Parker, address to the International Association of Chiefs of Police, Los Angeles, September 1952.

10. William Parker, address to the 1951 graduating class, Los Angeles Police Academy, April 1951.

11. Parker, *Parker on Police,* 69–70; William Parker, "Invasion from Within," speech delivered at the meeting of the National Automatic Merchandising Association, Chicago, September 1952; Parker, address to the 1951 graduating class.

12. Parker, *Parker on Police,* 49.

13. William Parker, address to the Legal Secretaries Association, Los Angeles, January 1951.

14. Critics of the police department have also charged that the height requirement provided a bureaucratic rationale for refusing to admit many women to the Academy.

15. Dominick, *To Protect and Serve,* 102. For a vivid picture of the LAPD Academy as a boot camp, see chapter 1 of Joseph Wambaugh's novel *The New Centurions.* Although Wambaugh, a former LAPD sergeant, captures much of the flavor of the LAPD (from analogies of Roman legions to general clannishness), and although his novels are among the most popular of the fictional depictions of the LAPD, he does not speak for the LAPD elites whose models I am discussing here, so I do not include his novels in my discussion.

16. Gates, *Chief,* 34–35. (Unless otherwise noted, all citations of Gates's *Chief* refer to page numbers in the 1992 edition of that book.)

17. Bhabha, *Location of Culture,* 86.

18. See Davis, *City of Quartz,* esp. chap.5; Sonenshein, *Politics in Black and White,* esp. chaps. 3 and 4; Herbert, *Policing Space,* esp. chaps. 1 and 8; Bryant et al., *Central Avenue Sounds.*

19. In 1970, the PDID was divided into two departments, the Organized Crime Intelligence Division and the Public Disorder Intelligence Division.

20. Webb, *The Badge,* 144–47. See also Gates, *Chief,* 71; Dominick, *To Protect and Serve,* 156.

21. In the words of the Chiefs Association: "Intelligence was seen as the gathering of as much information as possible to fit seemingly irrelevant facts into an overall pattern. Because it was often impossible during the initial gathering stages to be certain how the information would eventually be used, intelligence officials felt it unwise to exclude any data." Quoted in Dominick, *To Protect and Serve,* 154–55.

22. Koppes and Black, *Hollywood Goes to War.*

23. Parker, "Invasion from Within."

24. A perfect example is provided in the opening moments of the *Dragnet* episode that aired for the first time on June 8, 1953. Friday's narration is accompanied by film of LAPD technicians and clerical staff processing large amounts of paperwork through complex machinery, after the opening establishing shots of Los Angeles City Hall and the entrance to LAPD headquarters (which at that time was located in the basement of City Hall): "LAPD Headquarters. A place of records and files. Mostly it's a place of machines. Machines to find one card in 10,000, to find one bullet in a million. Machines to find the truth . . . and to find a lie. Radio to talk across the nation . . . or across the city. All these machines and the people behind them work twenty-four hours a day for one reason: to protect the citizens. That's my job too. I'm a cop." As time went on, Friday introduced more facts about the city as a whole (demographic information, crime rates, employment rates, miles of road, state of public information, historical data), but the basic format of the introduction remained the same. Parker, appalled at the use of the word *cop,* which he considered derisive slang, demanded only one change in the introductory format; after the first month of television production, Webb changed his concluding line to "That's my job. I carry a badge."

25. The most jarring example of Webb's narrative control is actually provided by Friday's partner, Frank Smith, in the episode that first aired on August 8, 1956. Two small girls are kidnapped, molested, and then recovered by police, and Friday and Smith are questioning the mother. She begins to cry: "If I told them that once, I've told them a thousand times: stay away from strangers! [she gulps] Oh! It must have been horrible for them! [she sobs]" When she says "horrible," Smith begins talking over her in monotone: "Yes ma'am did the girls tell you anything about the truck the man was driving?" The mother stops in mid-sob, sighs, and begins speaking in a clear, emotionless voice, eventually providing the clue that breaks the case.

26. "'[Webb] duplicated everything,' former LAPD Chief Tom Reddin would later recall. 'When you walked on a *Dragnet* set that was supposed to be a replica of the police-business office, you could bet it was an exact replica.' He made a plaster cast of a rock used as a paperweight in an LAPD office and then used it in the duplicated office on the set. He re-created a door to precisely resemble one at City Hall, going to great lengths to copy both its heavy brass hinges and the exact thump of that particular door. And, of course, there was always a technical advisor right there on the set showing them the correct procedures, and how things were done." Dominick, *To Protect and Serve,* 124.

27. Gabler, *Winchell*, 477.

28. Webb's 1954 movie *Dragnet* has several characteristics of film noir. At the film's conclusion, for example, just as Friday and Smith finally collect enough evidence to arrest a local gang boss, the suspect dies during a cancer operation. In the film's last shot, Friday tosses the key piece of evidence—a note—into the gutter, and we watch as the rain destroys it. The ending suggests a popular and unemulable noir theme—the futility of human striving—but this is completely alien to the rest of Webb's work, and I would argue that from Webb's perspective, justice has been done in the end of the film, even if Friday was not the one to carry it out. Webb used several noir conventions, but his attempts to "humanize" Friday never reached the point of positing that Friday's striving was futile in general, even if it was at times frustrated.

29. This episode, which first aired on June 17, 1957, does place Friday within a larger narrative context than most other episodes do, however. When Friday makes an extended report to his superior, the superior assumes the narrative position usually held by Friday, responding with sentence fragments to draw out Friday's statements. Friday also has to navigate one encounter with a character who employs a different but not inferior mode of professionalism: a hard-boiled physician who insists on seeing his patients alone rather than with a police escort.

30. Dominick, *To Protect and Serve*, 181.

31. William Parker, remarks made on *Meet the Press*, August 29, 1965.

32. The problem with the Watts community, Parker said on *Newsmaker* on August 14, 1965, was "false prophets": "We had the rule of law pretty well established at one time until they began to be preached to that the police were their enemies. . . . These people that represent these individuals through their organizations, now we would assume that they have some influence on them or they wouldn't be representing them. . . . I'm afraid we were influenced somewhat by these pseudo-leaders."

33. Parker asserted that the Mexican Americans in East Los Angeles were "just one step removed from the wild tribes of Mexico." See Davis, *City of Quartz*, 295.

34. Quoted in *Time*, August 27, 1965.

35. Parker, remarks on *Meet the Press*, August 29, 1965.

36. William Parker, remarks made on *Newsmaker*, August 14, 1965.

37. Ibid.

38. Indeed, Friday's attempts to speak the language of other citizens sound absurd: "Now, we've been rapping about 'doing our own thing.' Well, I'm doing my own thing. Keeping the faith, baby. With the people of this city." Episode first aired April 2, 1970.

39. Friday's speeches are increasingly contemptuous in such episodes, and he literally engages in finger-pointing. In the episode first aired on October 7, 1969, a patrolman complains to Friday that the LAPD "bends over backwards" for ethnic groups and comments that "they have problems, but they're *their* problems, not ours." Friday jabs his finger in the other man's direction and says, "That's where you're *dead* wrong, fella! They're our problems. We're policemen." Similarly, in the episode for September 15, 1967, Friday questions a Nazi who planted dynamite under an integrated

school. When the Nazi sneers, "I know my rights! You need to know a lot more! Like motive," Friday says: "Hate'll do. Try to wrap that walnut-sized brain around this, mister. You keep complaining about minorities." The Nazi responds, "So?" and Friday replies, "So, you're a psycho. They're a minority too."

40. The event that Evans defuses is actually far from a race riot. Evans breaks up a fight between a young white man and a young black man. The African American, a "pseudoleader" who has tried to talk Evans's audience out of joining the LAPD, claims that the white man treated him in a racist manner, but his girlfriend reports that he actually attacked the white man in a fit of jealousy. Evans succeeds in bringing the young men together by making fun of the girlfriend ("My daddy told me you never yell at a woman until you've got one; then you've *got* to yell to make yourself heard!"), and it is this success in race relations that makes him decide to stay on the force. Compare Webb's belittling of the idea of a "race riot" here with Parker's insistence in remarks made on *Meet the Press* and to the *Los Angeles Times* that he "did not consider [Watts] a race riot, since all the rioters were Negroes."

41. For example, in the episode that first aired on April 2, 1970, Friday tells his "sensitivity training" classmates, "We arrest them [drug dealers] and the courts don't see fit to convict them"; and in the episode for August 12, 1969, Friday snarls at a "hippie" suspect, "You've got *rights* mister, you dig? And we *sure* wouldn't want to see them violated, *would we?* Book him, and don't forget to read him his *rights.*" When Gannon comments on this relatively unusual show of passion, Friday says that he remembers the suspect from an earlier crime: "Two years ago the judge let him go because he claimed he didn't understand his *rights.*"

42. Davis's paranoia underscores the fact that he seems to have been opposed to any form of citizen political action. Davis was generally hostile to any citizen relationship with the force, for example, despite his sponsorship of a limited "community policing" program. Certain that he had no public support, the new chief lashed out at members of the "counterculture" and the "establishment" alike. Davis allied himself with the House Un-American Activities Committee to argue that a large number of elites in Los Angeles were members of the Communist Party. In a series of speeches and op-ed pieces in the *Los Angeles Times* and the *Herald-Examiner,* Davis lashed out at clergymen, "swimming pool communists," judges, and members of the Nixon administration. See, for example, "Reds Seek to Use Latin Youths as 'Prison Fodder,' Davis Says," *Los Angeles Times,* January 15, 1971; Davis's op-ed piece on capital punishment in the *Times,* February 26, 1971; and Davis's open letter to the Honorable Charles A. Loring, presiding judge of the Los Angeles Superior Court, which he distributed to the news media on January 30, 1972. Davis's attacks, and his insistence on the LAPD's superior position vis-à-vis other citizens of Los Angeles and other elites, fueled his political isolation from the conservative elements that supported Parker. After charging that crime in Los Angeles was the result of the Los Angeles Superior Court's being lax in its use of the death penalty, Davis was officially censured by the Bar Association. When Attorney General John Mitchell indicted several LAPD officers for abuse of authority, Davis argued that the Nixon administration was a pawn of

the "Eastern establishment" and the ACLU. During Davis's tenure, the LAPD continued the posture Parker adopted after Watts, becoming more militaristic and politically isolationist than it had been since Parker was hired in 1950.

43. Gates, *Chief,* 30.

44. Ibid., chap. 3. As Dominick recounts: "'Now look at him,' Bill Parker would sometimes urge his audience as he interrupted one of his countless speeches and pointed to Daryl Gates. 'Stand up now,' he'd say to Gates. 'I want you to stand up!' And Daryl Gates would stand up. 'This,' Parker would say, 'is a *policeman.* . . . Look at him!'" Dominick, *To Protect and Serve,* 247.

45. Quoted in Dominick, *To Protect and Serve,* 247.

46. Gates, *Chief,* 34–35.

47. Ibid., 31–32.

48. Gates, for example, writes: "People who spotted a police officer standing over a motorist . . . instinctively identified with the motorist. . . . At times it made you want to scream, 'Yeah, well, you should see where that cop is right now, buster. Down in the gutter somewhere, rolling around in the dirt with some scumbag. Seeing things you never have to see.'" Ibid., 47.

49. Quoted in *Los Angeles Times,* December 25, 1986; Dominick, *To Protect and Serve,* 327.

50. Gates, *Chief,* 330–31.

51. Ibid., 88–104. Gates relates: "They ringed their black-and-whites around my car—talk about circling the wagons—and their very presence, standing there, shotguns poised, became effective in turning people back. . . . For all his good intentions, it was impossible for Parker to visualize how widespread and out of control the rioting had grown. . . . 'Turn that radio off,' I snapped at Morrison, thinking, *Forgive me, Chief, but I have to turn you off.*" Ibid., 96–99.

52. Ibid., 110.

53. Dominick, *To Protect and Serve,* 262.

54. Gates, *Chief,* 121.

55. Ibid., 136.

56. Koppes and Black, *Hollywood Goes to War,* chap. 9.

57. Gates, *Chief,* 139. In the mid-1970s, Gates's office collaborated on the television show *S.W.A.T.* The show had some success, but it was a far cry from the 1950s *Dragnet,* commanding respectable but not outstanding ratings and having a style indistinguishable from the many other police dramas on the air at that time. The short-lived 2003 version of *Dragnet* (ABC) is a similar case; despite the borrowing of some of Webb's narrative devices, the show was clearly wedded to the police procedural style of producer Dick Wolf, not the ideology of L.A. Police Chief William Bratton.

58. Compare Gates's juxtaposition of his own elite "marine corps" and the "enemy armies" of the L.A. streets with Machiavelli's arguments for citizen armies in *The Art of War:* "Weapons borne by citizens or subjects, given by the laws and well regulated, never do damage; on the contrary, they are always an advantage, and cities keep themselves uncorrupted longer by means of these weapons than without them." A tyrant,

on the other hand, should disarm the people of a city "in order to command them more easily" (578). Unlike Fabrizio, Machiavelli's partisan of citizen militias who "condemns those who in their actions do not imitate the ancients," Gates was concerned with the population of Los Angeles only insofar as he could "command them more easily." Again, Machiavelli suggests why: "A city that uses its own forces, fears only its own citizens" (585). See Machiavelli, *The Art of War*, 572–90.

59. Quoted in *Los Angeles Times*, April 7, 1989; see also Davis, *City of Quartz*, 267. "Suspected gang member" became an increasingly broad classification under Gates. In cooperation with City Attorney James Hahn, the LAPD included entire neighborhoods containing suspected gangsters and the family members of suspected gangsters (as well as the majority of young African American men in L.A.) under the umbrella of criminal suspects. Indeed, Hahn attempted to detain three hundred black teenagers on charges such as "congregating in groups of two or more" and "remaining in public streets for more than five minutes at any time of day or night." See Davis, *City of Quartz*, 268–71, 277–84. Hahn was elected mayor of Los Angeles in 2001, with the support of the Los Angeles African American community, but has since alienated many blacks and LAPD officers through his bruising fights with departing LAPD Chief Bernard Parks.

60. Gates, *Chief*, 286–87.

61. Quoted in *Los Angeles Times*, April 3, 1988; see Davis, *City of Quartz*, 268. Local elites, such as the chief of the Los Angeles District Attorney's Hardcore Drug Unit and the mayor of Artesia, were more specific about the conflict: "This is Vietnam here," gangs are "the Viet Cong abroad in our society," comparable to "the murderous militias of Beirut." See also Davis, *City of Quartz*, 277–92; Dominick, *To Protect and Serve*, 309–58; Gates, *Chief*, 265–98.

62. Gates discusses the uprising in the 1994 paperback edition of *Chief*: "The anti-LAPD mood of the city, which had engulfed the department since the Rodney King incident, served as a backdrop against which we had to operate. For fourteen months officers were under attack from citizens and political leaders alike.... Privately, many officers told me they decided using force wasn't worth it.... To an extent the tugging and pulling of the community did affect me. I was being attacked on all sides, from the media, the Christopher Commission [which issued the report on abuses within the LAPD] and the Westside liberals, to the people in South Central who claimed police brutality.... I was under siege from a citywide budget deficit and from the constant berating of the department on the whole use-of-force issue." Gates argues that this might have slowed LAPD reaction or discouraged officers from acting. He also posits that a commander and a captain of the LAPD at the riot's starting point, both African American, "may have been influenced by some of our black leaders who pleaded caution" (440–44). Thus, in Gates's view, bad leaders, clannishness, and an unworthy citizenry made up the causes for the LAPD's withdrawal at the height of the fighting.

63. Gates, *Chief*, 223, 274.

64. Vernon, *L.A. Justice*, chaps. 16–22, esp. pp. 190–91, 205, 223. Vernon writes: "An

overemphasis on the material is a terrible evil, a subtle deadly diversion from the people in our lives and our needs. . . . Children observe the role models around them. When they see their parents value material things over them, they don't feel good about themselves" (193).

65. Ibid., 134, 182, 254.

66. Ibid., 58–59.

67. Ibid., 80–81.

68. Ibid., 81.

69. Ibid., 59, 181–83, 185–99, 237–52. Indeed, when Vernon shifts from the account of his childhood and returns to the story of his adult life in the LAPD, he begins by telling the reader that the Police Commission staff room is stocked with "a box of oatmeal and chocolate chip cookies, the kind I can't resist" (65). Even as assistant chief, Vernon holds on to his childlike place within the proper chain of authority.

4. MORE THAN HUMAN

1. Paine, *Common Sense,* 51.

2. Silverman, "Back to the Future," 109.

3. Ibid., 114.

4. The accused officers were Stacey Koon, Laurence Powell, Timothy Wind, and Theodore Briseno.

5. The career of adopted favorite son Ronald Reagan provides overwhelming evidence of the way this fantasy has become fact; and facts are, as Reagan pointed out, stubborn things.

6. See Rogin, "The Sword Became a Flashing Vision," in *Ronald Reagan;* Rogin, *Blackface, White Noise,* esp. 73–156.

7. See, for example, "One Man Slain; Pool Hunted for Body," and "Girls Quizzed about Hoodlums," both in *Los Angeles Herald-Examiner,* August 3, 1942; "150 Rounded Up in Killing, Gang Terror," *Los Angeles Herald-Examiner,* August 4, 1942; "Marijuana Orgies before Terror Sorties Bared in Gang Roundup," *Los Angeles Herald-Examiner,* August 4, 1942; "Zoot Suiters Learn Lesson in Fight with Servicemen," *Los Angeles Times,* June 8, 1943; "Reds Seek to Use Latin Youths as 'Prison Fodder,' Davis Says," *Los Angeles Times,* January 15, 1971.

8. See Bhabha, *Location of Culture,* 85–94.

9. William Parker, remarks made on *Newsmaker,* August 14, 1965.

10. Sonenshein, *Politics in Black and White,* 80, 141–43. Sonenshein notes, "In fact, the far more open opposition of the incumbent regime in Los Angeles helped further cement relations between Blacks and white reformers" (71).

11. Ibid., 143.

12. Ibid., 156.

13. Ibid., 161, 221, 224–26.

14. Ibid., 184. Here Sonenshein is adapting Fred Greenstein's interpretation of Dwight D. Eisenhower's presidential style.

15. Ibid., passim.

16. Davis, *City of Quartz,* esp. chaps. 1 and 4. See also Davis's discussion of Hahn's tenure as city attorney in chapter 5; and the book's prologue, in which Davis explicitly argues that the "best place to view Los Angeles of the next millennium is from the ruins of its alternative future" (3).

17. Ibid., 138.

18. See Ibid., chap. 2, esp. 138–44.

19. Ibid., 82.

20. Warner Brothers found the original cut confusing, so the studio added some scenes, removed others, and recorded an explanatory voice-over narration.

21. Their idyllic forest is not even part of the film's world; the footage of their car is actually clipped from the opening of Stanley Kubrick's *The Shining* (1980). The protagonists have merely escaped into another director's nightmare.

22. Machiavelli, *The Prince,* chap. 14, p. 57. Cicero, *On the Commonwealth,* II.42, 193.

BIBLIOGRAPHY

Adams, John. *The Political Writings of John Adams.* Edited by George Peek. New York: Macmillan, 1954.

Arendt, Hannah. *On Revolution.* New York: Penguin, 1963.

Baum, L. Frank. *The Wonderful Wizard of Oz.* Edited by Peter Glassman. London: Justin Knowles, 1987.

Behlmer, Rudy, ed. *Inside Warner Brothers (1935–1951).* New York: Viking, 1985.

Bhabha, Homi K. *The Location of Culture.* New York: Routledge, 1994.

Brownlow, Kevin. *The Parade's Gone By . . . .* New York: Ballantine, 1968.

Bryant, Clora, Buddy Collette, William Green, Steven Isoardi, Jack Kelson, Horace Tapscott, Gerald Wilson, and Marl Young. *Central Avenue Sounds: Jazz in Los Angeles.* Berkeley: University of California Press, 1998.

Burns, William J. *The Masked War: The Story of a Peril That Threatened the United States by the Man Who Uncovered the Dynamite Conspirators and Sent Them to Jail.* New York: George H. Doran, 1913.

Ceplair, Larry, and Steven Englund. *The Inquisition in Hollywood: Politics in the Film Community, 1930–60.* Berkeley: University of California Press, 1979.

Cicero, Marcus Tullius. *On the Commonwealth.* Translated by George Holland Sabine and Stanley Barney Smith. New York: Macmillan, 1976.

Davis, Margaret Leslie. *Rivers in the Desert: William Mulholland and the Inventing of Los Angeles.* New York: HarperCollins, 1993.

Davis, Mike. *City of Quartz: Excavating the Future in Los Angeles.* New York: Vintage, 1990.

Dominick, Joe. *To Protect and Serve: The LAPD's Century of War in the City of Dreams.* New York: Pocket Books, 1994.

Escobar, Edward J. *Race, Police, and the Making of a Political Identity: Mexican Americans and the Los Angeles Police Department, 1900–1945.* Berkeley: University of California Press, 1999.

Fliegelman, Jay. *Declaring Independence: Jefferson, Natural Language, and the Culture of Performance*. Stanford, CA: Stanford University Press, 1993.

Franklin, Benjamin. *Autobiography*. New York: Penguin, 1986.

Friedrich, Otto. *City of Nets: A Portrait of Hollywood in the 1940s*. New York: Perennial, 1986.

Gabler, Neal. *An Empire of Their Own: How the Jews Invented Hollywood*. New York: Doubleday Anchor, 1988.

Gabler, Neal. *Winchell: Gossip, Power, and the Culture of Celebrity*. New York: Knopf, 1994.

Gates, Daryl. *Chief: My Life in the LAPD*. New York: Bantam, 1992. (Paperback ed., 1994)

Glassman, Peter. Afterword to *The Wonderful Wizard of Oz*, by L. Frank Baum. London: Justin Knowles, 1987.

Gottlieb, Robert, and Irene Wolt. *Thinking Big: The Story of the "Los Angeles Times," Its Publishers, and Its Influence over Southern California*. New York: G. P. Putnam's Sons, 1977.

Hamilton, Ian. *Writers in Hollywood 1915–1951*. New York: Carroll & Graf, 1990.

Hampton, Benjamin. *History of the American Film Industry from Its Beginnings to 1931*. New York: Dover, 1978.

Havelock, Eric A. *Preface to Plato*. Cambridge, MA: Belknap, 1963.

Herbert, Steve. *Policing Space: Territoriality and the Los Angeles Police Department*. Minneapolis: University of Minnesota Press, 1997.

Higham, Charles. *Merchant of Dreams: Louis B. Mayer, MGM, and the Secret Hollywood*. New York: Donald I. Fine, 1993.

Hindle, Brooke. *Emulation and Innovation*. New York: New York University Press, 1981.

Honig, Bonnie. *Political Theory and the Displacement of Politics*. Ithaca, NY: Cornell University Press, 1993.

Jackson, Helen Hunt. *Ramona: A Life*. New York: Signet, 2002.

Jaeger, Werner. *Paideia*. Oxford: Oxford University Press, 1967.

Kahrl, William. *Water and Power: The Conflict over Los Angeles' Water Supply in the Owens Valley*. Berkeley: University of California Press, 1982.

Karnes, David Alan. "Modern Metropolis: Mass Culture and the Transformation of Los Angeles 1890–1950." Ph.D. diss., University of California, Berkeley, 1991.

Koppes, Clayton, and Gregory Black. *Hollywood Goes to War: How Politics, Profits, and Propaganda Shaped World War II Movies*. Berkeley: University of California Press, 1987.

Lear, Jackson. *No Place of Grace: Antimodernism and the Transformation of American Culture, 1880–1920*. Chicago: University of Chicago Press, 1994.

Lincoln, Abraham. *The Political Thought of Abraham Lincoln*. Edited by Richard Current. New York: Macmillan, 1985.

Livy. *The History of Rome from Its Foundation*. Translated by Aubrey Selincourt. London: Penguin, 1960.

Machiavelli, Niccolo. *The Art of War.* Translated by Allan Gilbert. Durham, NC: Duke University Press, 1989.

Machiavelli, Niccolo. *Discourses on the First Decade of Titus Livius.* Translated by Allan Gilbert. Durham, NC: Duke University Press, 1989.

Machiavelli, Niccolo. *The Prince.* Translated by Allan Gilbert. Durham, NC: Duke University Press, 1989.

McWilliams, Carey. *Southern California: An Island on the Land.* Salt Lake City, UT: Peregrine Smith, 1946.

Miller, Richard Connelly. "Otis and His *Times:* The Career of Harrison Gray Otis." Ph.D. diss., University of California, Berkeley, 1961.

Mitchell, Greg. *Campaign of the Century: Upton Sinclair's Race for Governor of California and the Birth of Media Politics.* New York: Random House, 1992.

Mowry, George E. *The California Progressives.* Berkeley: University of California Press, 1951.

Otis, Harrison Gray. *Story of the Distinct Victory over Militant and Despotic Trades-Unionism Won by the "Los Angeles Times" in a Sixteen Years' Battle: Showing the Virtue of Standing Fast.* Los Angeles: Times-Mirror, 1907.

Otis, Harrison Gray. "Milestones, Marking Some High Spots in the Pathway of a Strenuous Life." Unpublished manuscript, *Los Angeles Times* Library, n.d.

Paine, Thomas. *Common Sense.* Indianapolis: Bobbs-Merrill, 1953.

Parker, William H. *Parker on Police.* Edited by O. W. Wilson. Los Angeles: Thomas, 1957.

Pitkin, Hanna. *Fortune Is a Woman: Gender and Politics in the Thought of Niccolo Machiavelli.* Berkeley: University of California Press, 1984.

Pitt, Leonard. *The Decline of the Californios.* Berkeley: University of California Press, 1966.

Plutarch. *Lives of Famous Greeks and Romans.* Translated by John Dryden and edited by Arthur Hugh Clough. New York: Modern Library, 1992.

Pocock, J. G. A. *The Machiavellian Moment: Florentine Political Thought and the Atlantic Republican Tradition.* Princeton, NJ: Princeton University Press, 1975.

Polan, Dana. *Power and Paranoia: History, Narrative, and the American Cinema, 1940–1950.* New York: Columbia University Press, 1986.

Ray, Robert. *The Avante Garde Finds Andy Hardy.* Cambridge, MA: Harvard University Press, 1995.

Roddick, Nick. *A New Deal in Entertainment: Warner Brothers in the 1930s.* London: British Film Institute, 1983.

Rogin, Michael. *Fathers and Children: Andrew Jackson and the Subjugation of the American Indian.* New York: Knopf, 1975.

Rogin, Michael. *Ronald Reagan, the Movie, and Other Episodes in Political Demonology.* Berkeley: University of California Press, 1987.

Rogin, Michael. *Blackface, White Noise: Jewish Immigrants in the Hollywood Melting Pot.* Berkeley: University of California Press, 1996.

Roosevelt, Franklin Delano. *FDR's Fireside Chats.* Edited by Russell D. Buhite and David W. Levy. New York: Penguin, 1993.

Rosten, Leo. *Hollywood: The Movie Colony, the Movie Makers.* New York: Harcourt, Brace, 1941.

Sanchez, Rosaura. *Telling Identities: The Californio Testimonios.* Minneapolis: University of Minnesota Press, 1995.

Schatz, Thomas. *The Genius of the System: Hollywood Filmmaking in the Studio Era.* New York: Pantheon, 1988.

Selznick, Irene Mayer. *A Private View.* New York: Knopf, 1983.

Silverman, Kaja. "Back to the Future." *Camera Obscura* 27 (1991): 108–33.

Slotkin, Richard. *The Fatal Environment: The Myth of the Frontier in the Age of Industrialization, 1800–1890.* Middletown, CT: Wesleyan University Press, 1985.

Sonenshein, Raphael. *Politics in Black and White: Race and Power in Los Angeles.* Princeton, NJ: Princeton University Press, 1993.

Starr, Kevin. *Inventing the Dream: California through the Progressive Era.* Oxford: Oxford University Press, 1985.

Starr, Kevin. *Material Dreams: Southern California through the 1920s.* Oxford: Oxford University Press, 1990.

Trachtenberg, Alan. *Incorporation of America: Culture and Society in the Gilded Age.* New York: Hill & Wang, 1982.

Tygiel, Jules. *The Great Los Angeles Swindle: Oil, Stocks, and Scandal during the Roaring Twenties.* Oxford: Oxford University Press, 1994.

Ulin, David L., ed. *Writing Los Angeles: A Literary Anthology.* New York: Library of America, 2002.

U.S. House of Representatives, Committee on Un-American Activities. *The House Committee on Un-American Activities: What It Is—What It Does.* Washington, DC: U.S. House of Representatives, 1958.

Vaniman, Roscoe J. "The Southern California Land Boom of 1887." Ph.D. diss., Claremont Graduate School, 1940.

Vernon, Bob. *L.A. Justice: Lessons from the Firestorm.* Los Angeles: Focus on the Family, 1993.

Webb, Jack. *The Badge.* New York: Prentice Hall, 1958.

Weems, Mason. *The Life of Washington.* Edited by Marcus Cunliffe. Cambridge, MA: Belknap, 1962.

Wills, Garry. *Cincinnatus: George Washington and the Enlightenment.* New York: Doubleday, 1984.

Wills, Garry. *Lincoln at Gettysburg: The Words That Remade America.* New York: Simon & Schuster, 1992.

Wilson, Woodrow. "The Ideals of America." *Atlantic Monthly,* December 1902.

Wood, Gordon. *The Creation of the American Republic 1776–1787.* New York: Norton, 1969.

Wood, Gordon. *The Radicalism of the American Revolution.* New York: Vintage, 1991.

Wyllie, Irvin. *The Self-Made Man in America.* New York: Free Press, 1954.

FILMOGRAPHY

Action in the North Atlantic. Directed by Lloyd Bacon. Warner Brothers Studios, 1943.

Andy Hardy Gets Spring Fever. Directed by W. S. Van Dyke II. MGM, 1939.

Andy Hardy Meets Debutante. Directed by George B. Seitz. MGM, 1940.

Angels with Dirty Faces. Directed by Michael Curtiz. Warner Brothers Studios, 1938.

Ben-Hur. Directed by Fred Niblo. MGM, 1925.

The Big Parade. Directed by King Vidor. MGM, 1925.

The Birth of a Nation. Directed by D. W. Griffith. 1915.

Blade Runner. Directed by Ridley Scott. Warner Brothers Studios/Alan Ladd Jr. Productions, 1982.

Casablanca. Directed by Michael Curtiz. Warner Brothers Studios, 1942.

Chinatown. Directed by Roman Polanski. Paramount Pictures, 1974.

Confessions of a Nazi Spy. Directed by Anatole Litvak. Warner Brothers Studios, 1939.

Dead End. Directed by William Wyler. Samuel Goldwyn, 1937.

Destination Tokyo. Directed by Delmer Daves. Warner Brothers Studios, 1943.

Dragnet. Directed by Jack Webb. Mark VII Limited, 1954.

42nd Street. Directed by Lloyd Bacon. Warner Brothers Studios, 1933.

Gone with the Wind. Directed by Victor Fleming. MGM/Selznick International, 1939.

Grand Hotel. Directed by Edmund Goulding. MGM, 1932.

A Guy Named Joe. Directed by Victor Fleming. MGM, 1943.

The Jazz Singer. Directed by Alan Crosland. Warner Brothers Studios, 1927.

Life Begins for Andy Hardy. Directed by George B. Seitz. MGM, 1941.

The Maltese Falcon. Directed by John Huston. Warner Brothers Studios, 1941.

Manhattan Melodrama. Directed by W. S. Van Dyke II. MGM, 1934.

The Mortal Storm. Directed by Frank Borzage. MGM, 1940.

Mrs. Miniver. Directed by William Wyler. MGM, 1942.

Mutiny on the Bounty. Directed by Frank Lloyd. MGM, 1935.

The Public Enemy. Directed by William A. Wellman. Warner Brothers Studios, 1931.

The Shining. Directed by Stanley Kubrick. Warner Brothers Studios, 1980.

Song of Russia. Directed by Gregory Ratoff. MGM, 1943.

The Spanish Earth. Directed by Joris Ivens. Herman Shumlin, 1937.

Tarzan the Ape Man. Directed by W. S. Van Dyke II. MGM, 1932.

The Thin Man. Directed by W. S. Van Dyke II. MGM, 1934.

Thirty Seconds over Tokyo. Directed by Mervyn LeRoy. MGM, 1944.

Trader Horn. Directed by W. S. Van Dyke II. MGM, 1931.

White Heat. Directed by Raoul Walsh. Warner Brothers Studios, 1949.

The Wizard of Oz. Directed by Victor Fleming. MGM, 1939.

INDEX

American Revolution, xvii, 1–3, 6, 59, 110–11

Andy Hardy series, 34–39, 54, 66, 114

Angels with Dirty Faces, 42–43

anti-Semitism, 49, 60n64, 64

Arendt, Hannah, xiii, xx, 60, 111

authority, xiii, 35–54, 60–62, 89, 94–98, 101, 111

Bhabha, Homi, xxiii–xxiv, 2, 11, 18–20, 26, 50, 54, 76, 97, 105, 112

blacklist in Hollywood, 62

Blade Runner, xxvii, 102–4, 109–10

Bogart, Humphrey, 44–45, 56–58, 62

Bradley, Tom, xxvii, 91, 104, 106–8, 109

Bradley Coalition, 106–8, 113

Cagney, James, 42–43, 64

California gubernatorial election (1934), 47

Californios, 2

Casablanca, 56–58

Chandler, Harry, xxi, 19–21, 24–26, 107

Chinatown, xi–xii, 24n72

Cicero, xiv–xv, 4–5, 26, 30

City of Quartz (Davis), xxvii, 108–9

Civil War, 2–3, 7, 9

Committee for the First Amendment, 62

Community Relations Council, 63

corruption, xiv, xxv, 18–20, 70–77, 87, 97

Davis, Ed, 89n42, 105

democratic pedagogy, xxviii, 60, 93–94, 113; in colonies, xii, xxvii, 15, 105; mimesis and, 66, 111

Dragnet, xxvi–xxvii, 78–83, 81n28, 86–89, 87n38, 88n39, 89n41, 93

emulation: as contest, 39, 52, 54, 60, 74; defined, xv; as exclusion, 26, 89; Harrison Gray Otis and, xxi, 3, 20; William Parker and, xxv–xxvi, 70, 72, 77–78; as *virtú,* xvi–xvii, 1, 50, 111

founding myths, xi

Gates, Daryl, xxvi–xxvii, 75, 89–98, 113; Tom Bradley and, 91, 107;

William Parker and, 89–91, 95; SWAT and, 92–93
Great Depression, 29, 38, 46–47, 56, 71

Hahn, James, 104, 108
Honig, Bonnie, xi, xx, xxvii–xxviii
HUAC (House Un-American Activities Committee), xxv, 112; in Hollywood, 60–65, 60n64, 107–8; LAPD and, 89n42, 96
imitation, 104; as anti-political strategy, 20, 50, 63, 95–96; as brainwashing, 61, 64, 96; *Dragnet* and, 86, 89; as piety, xv–xvi, 35, 37, 39
innovation, xiv, xvi, xviii, 4–5, 26, 30

King, Rodney, 91, 95, 98, 108, 113

LAPD, xxv–xxvii, 14, 69–71, 113; as an army, 75, 76, 91–95; emulation of, 73–76, 81; as exemplary, 70, 72–75; Daryl Gates and, 89–98; media and, 77–78, 82–83, 86–89, 93n57; William Parker and, 71–86, 97–99; race and, 84, 85, 94, 105–7
Los Angeles: as a dystopia, xxvii, 102, 108–10; founding of, xi; as a mimetic utopia, xxviii, 102; refounding of, xx–xxi, 3, 9, 69; as a Spanish village, xi, xxi, 2–3, 20, 25
Los Angeles mayoral election (1911), 18–20
Los Angeles Times, xxiii, 7–27, 47, 106, 114; bombing of, 16–17; LAPD and, 77, 94, 105; mimesis and, xxi; Harrison Gray Otis and, 7, 10, 13–18, 24
Los Angeles uprising (1992), xxvi, 95–96, 108
Lincoln, Abraham, xviii–xx, 6–8, 24, 39, 50, 111
Love, Eulia, 92

M&M (Merchants and Manufacturers' Association), 13–16, 18, 23, 46, 63, 130
Machiavelli, Niccolo, xiii–xiv, xxv, 4, 50, 69, 113; *Discourses*, xiv, 8, 73
Maltese Falcon, The, 44–45
Mayer, Louis B., 30–40, 66; founding of MGM Studios, 31–32; Haverhill, Massachusetts; and 31, 32, 36; opposition to leftist politics and, 46–47, 104–5; Republican Party and, 33–34, 33n15; World War II and, 51–55, 58
media, xx, 29; mimesis and, 77, 101
MGM (Metro-Goldwyn-Mayer Studios), 30, 42–43, 66; as an exemplary studio, 32–34, 32n5; mimesis and, 36, 39–40; World War II and, 51–55
mimesis, xiv–xvi; as colonial strategy, xxiii, xxv, 11, 54, 86, 112; as entertainment, 35, 39–40, 49, 78–83; as policing, 63, 66, 94, 96; as reportage, xx–xxi, 50, 80–81, 101–2
Motion Picture Association for the Preservation of American Ideals, 60, 104
Mrs. Miniver, 52–56
Mulholland, William, 20–24, 23n66, 23n67, 91

Nye, Senator Gerald: propaganda subcommittee, 48–49, 52, 64

"open shop" in Los Angeles, 11–13, 15–16, 20, 26, 104
organized labor, 104–5; in Hollywood, 33, 47–47; war for "Otistown" and, 12–20
Otis, Harrison Gray, 6–26, 104–6, 111–13; Civil War and, 7–9; corruption and, 18–19, 24; emulation and,

8–9, 20, 26; *Los Angeles Times* and, 7–25; M&M and, 13–15, 18; mimesis and, 15, 20, 26, 86, 97; organized labor and, 11–20, 46; refounding of Los Angeles and, xxi–xxiv, 9, 73; Republican Party and, 6–7, 18, 24; Spanish-American war and, 11, 15
Owens Valley aqueduct, 18, 23
OWI (Office of War Information), 50–52, 55, 93, 108, 126

Parker, William, xxv–xxvi, 67, 69–86, 113; civic education and policing, 72–73, 76, 78; corruption and, 73–76, 78; emulation and, xxv, 72–74, 77, 83, 91; Daryl Gates and 89–90; LAPD and 71–86; race and, 84–85, 94, 105–6; television and, 77, 83; Watts uprising and, 83–86, 92
Parker Center, ix, 99
PDID (Public Disorder Information Division), 76, 77, 95–96
Philippines, the, xxii, 3, 11, 15, 26, 73, 105
PID (Public Information Division), 77, 80
Pitkin, Hanna, 1, 9, 26
Popular Front, the, xxiv, 48, 55, 58, 62
"proactive policing," 75, 76, 84, 90
propaganda, 48–52, 54, 60–63; defined, 50

race, xxvii; as a political category, 105–8, 105n7; LAPD and, 71, 71n3, 76, 84–85, 88, 88n40, 89n42, 94
Rankin, John, 60, 64, 65
Reagan administration, 94, 107
refounding, xx–xxi, 3, 6, 9, 25, 29, 69, 73, 113
Rogin, Michael, 3–4, 15, 29, 101, 105
Rome, xiv–xv, 91, 111; as metaphor, 3, 54, 74

Roosevelt administration, xxiv, 27, 30, 47–48, 50, 52, 55, 60–61

San Fernando Valley, 18, 21, 24, 85
San Pedro Harbor, 9–10
"self-made man," xviii, 3, 30, 64, 111; Tom Bradley and, 106; defined, 4; economic model of, 5, 25; emulation and, xxiii, 4–6, 15, 20; Harrison Gray Otis and, 6–16, 20–25, 26
slavery, 6–7; as metaphor, 8, 12, 15, 59, 104
Sleepy Lagoon, 71
"small town virtue," 30, 32, 37, 39, 59
Southern Pacific Railroad, 8–10
Spanish-American War, 11, 54, 59, 111
SWAT (Special Weapons and Tactics team), 92–93, 93n57

television, xxvi, 66, 77–78, 86–89, 93, 96
Thalberg, Irving, 33–35, 34n16, 39–40, 47
Thomas, J. Parnell, 64, 64n77, 66

U.S. Congress, 10, 48–49, 60–61

Vernon, Bob, 96–97, 97n69
virtú, xiv, xx, 9, 64, 114

war as metaphor for Los Angeles, 9, 108–9; according to Harrison Gray Otis, 11–19, 26; according to the LAPD, 84, 91–95
Warner, Harry, 41–43, 61n68, 66; testimony to the Nye propaganda subcommittee, 49–50
Warner, Jack, 41, 66; HUAC and, 60
Warner Brothers Studios, 30, 40–45, 66; and organized labor, 46–47; and the Roosevelt administration, 46; and World War II, 55–58

Watts uprising, xxvi, 83–86, 91, 105–6
Webb, Jack, xi–xii, xxviii, 69; as
    allegorical representation of
    "authority," 88–89; and *Dragnet,*
    78–83, 86–89; and film noir, 81–82,
    81n28; and mimesis, xxvi, 79–81;
    on William Parker, 71n4, 76; and
    race, 88

White Heat, 64
Wilson, Woodrow, xxi–xxii, 15, 112
Wizard of Oz, The, 39–42
World War II, 45–60, 70–71, 78, 93;
    Hollywood studios and, 45, 48–61;
    William Parker and, 71, 76
"zoot suit riots," 71

Ronald J. Schmidt Jr. is assistant professor of political science at the University of Southern Maine. He has also taught courses in political theory, urban politics, and the politics of race and ethnicity at Dartmouth College and Smith College.